Collected Poems

Born in rural Cheshire in 1944 David Chaloner spent his early years dreaming of escape. As the closest city, Manchester provided a cultural and social context for his early writing, when jazz was available in clubs created from empty cotton warehouses and Granada Television struggled with the idea of a new arts programme that included poetry. Apart from 'Little Press' publication, the first published work appeared in the Tandem paperback *Generation X*, a true sociological record of the times, and the Penguin anthology, *Children of Albion*. In the late sixties he founded *ONE*, a magazine for new writing, that existed through the transitional years of a move to London in the early seventies. A continuing sense of enquiry and curiosity informs his work and helps in pushing the possibilities of language, music and image in varying and divers ways.

Collected Poems

David Chaloner

CAMBRIDGE

PUBLISHED BY SALT PUBLISHING
PO Box 937, Great Wilbraham, Cambridge PDO CB1 5JX United Kingdom

All rights reserved

© David Chaloner, 2005

The right of David Chaloner to be identified as the
author of this work has been asserted by him in accordance
with Section 77 of the Copyright, Designs and Patents Act 1988.

This book is in copyright. Subject to statutory exception
and to provisions of relevant collective licensing agreements,
no reproduction of any part may take place without the written
permission of Salt Publishing.

First published 2005

Printed and bound in the United Kingdom by Lightning Source

Typeset in Swift 9.5 / 13

*This book is sold subject to the conditions that it shall not,
by way of trade or otherwise, be lent, re-sold, hired out,
or otherwise circulated without the publisher's prior consent
in any form of binding or cover other than that in which
it is published and without a similar condition including this
condition being imposed on the subsequent purchaser.*

ISBN 1 876857 75 7 paperback

SP

1 3 5 7 9 8 6 4 2

For those I love

Contents

UNCOLLECTED EARLY POEMS ... 1
  Wish You Were Here ... 3
  "Tonight the glass is filled frequently . . ." ... 4
  "white flakes peel from the wall . . ." ... 5
  Vesalii Icones (Andreas Vesalius: De Humani Corporis Fabrica) ... 6
  "I cannot move . . ." ... 10
  "disappearance is rendered more terrible
    for being so complete . . ." ... 11
  Going Out For Cigarettes ... 12
  Poem for Mary ... 13
  "a quick gesture attracts my attention . . ." ... 14
  The Photographs ... 15
  "because you are . . ." ... 16
  "this place . . ." ... 17
  "leaning over . . ." ... 18
  "you do not believe in the definition of wall . . ." ... 19
  "let us say that by his presence he intimidates . . ." ... 20
  "he adapts to the inertia in the room . . ." ... 21
  "there are times . . ." ... 22

DARK PAGES SLOW TURNS BRIEF SALVES (1969) ... 23
  "it is . . ." ... 25
  "the day slips . . ." ... 26
  "star gazer . . ." ... 27
  "I speak of one . . ." ... 28
  "you are . . ." ... 29
  "so we watch him totter . . ." ... 30
  "that speech gags the mouth & words sleep . . ." ... 31
  "not simply this . . ." ... 32

"take..."	33
"such gleanings..."	34
"delicately..."	35
"not that..."	36
"lady..."	37
"horde..."	38
"an exorcism..."	39
"the folds..."	40
Gift	41
"awake to your savagery as you rent the turf's..."	42
"the window..."	43
"oyster-catchers throng the striated shore..."	44
"do we speak of the metaphor..."	45
"we make the silence..."	46
"journeys wld be the measure..."	47
"usually it's early morning..."	48
"wld say it thus..."	49
"rooks from the trees black as the..."	51
"the wild duck..."	52
"broken line traces out condition..."	54
for David Sims	55
against wall	56
"a child stamps its foot..."	57
"what "time" could dispel..."	58
A Personal Poem	59
"moving round you the sun its axis the sun..."	61
Sunlight	63
"did I say from here we can hear..."	64
YEAR OF METEORS (1972)	65
"Five hours of darkness fill the window..."	67

Breakfast	68
Twice	69
"voices flap deviously..."	70
The Hotel Temporary	71
"From Walt Whitman..."	72
"broken ornaments..."	73
"you walk through the door and a year passes..."	74
"it becomes a monday morning inside the clock..."	75
"an incoming tide..."	76
"fatigue creeps closer under the awning..."	77
CHOCOLATE SAUCE (1973)	79
"a pattern emerges..."	81
Swirl	82
"sunlight slants in through the window..."	83
"the problem the grass under the saplings..."	84
"he is exploring the inertia of the room..."	85
"move..."	86
"to go adrift seemingly given extra time to receive..."	87
Itch	88
The Situation	89
The Photographs	90
Domestic Scenes	91
"a landslide carries the background from sight..."	92
Racers	93
Exercise	94
"not merely false starts..."	95
Texture	96
"the patrons sip their drinks..."	97
"as we drive back today from yesterday..."	98
"surf falls noisily along the tunnel of half-closed..."	99

"recently having returned from a long journey..."	100
"and the nets hung on..."	101
"your arrival is delayed in the public address system..."	102
"instinctively advances towards adventure..."	103
Visiting	104
The Cast in Order of Appearance	105
"hard trees shake furtively..."	106
Coda	107
Dilemma	108
Doors	109
"undisclosed destinations lurk in benzedrine timetables..."	110
"the ramp gives us a new idea..."	111
"the notes tell of earlier occasions..."	112
The Swimming-Pool Saga	113
"you do not believe in the wall..."	114
"before sleep you notice..."	115
"standing in open space confidently..."	116
"dear reader this was to have been a letter..."	117
Cameo	118
"the former arbiter cruises slowly..."	119
"a cleaned-out sensation passes around the room..."	120

PROJECTIONS (1977)   121

"the first restless flaws of morning..."	123
Changes	125
"technology idles below the window..."	126
Travelling	127
"sparked off more than once before..."	128
Introductions	129
Holidays	130
Interior : Morning	131

Ronny's Friend	132
"each day is necessary and sustains..."	133
TODAY BACKWARDS (1977)	135
Foxtrot Marathon	137
"sitting here how do they know where..."	138
"a sense of strain between times is outlandish..."	139
"fortunately there is a method, you suppose..."	140
"the sky suggests the sundry forces..."	142
"how restless they are..."	143
"the hush that pervades..."	144
"the swarthy ripples of her finger-tips..."	145
"does the idea of language leave an impression..."	146
"a tight lipped aurora..."	147
"then it seemed that all our efforts led back..."	148
"this evening I am entertained by a blackbird..."	149
Battledore & Shuttlecock	150
"lost oddments provoke moments of doubt..."	151
"there is enough for us all..."	152
Today Backwards	153
FADING INTO BRILLIANCE (1978)	155
Fading Into Brilliance	157
The Adventure	160
The Spring-Loaded Cash Drawer	163
Getting Through The Door	165
Static Journey	167
An Adventurous Episode Rejected By Boys Own Paper	168
Nothing Is Abstract	172
The Strategy	174
Risks	176
Second Chance	178

Examining The Earthworks	179
Never Let It End	180
The Last Pages	182
HOTEL ZINGO (1981)	187
Debate	189
"Unable to ignore . . ."	190
The News	191
"Mist loiters throughout the afternoon . . ."	192
Sitting on the Sidelines	193
"the bowl of marigolds on the cabinet . . ."	194
"Who remains to recall such afternoons . . ."	195
"the surrounding area prepares itself . . ."	197
Incredible Vistas	198
Sun House Propaganda	199
The Preparations	200
"All the alternatives unite and place their complex proposal . . ."	202
Exercise for One Leg	203
Occupying Absence	204
January	206
Deliberate Modulations	208
Personal Choice	210
"There is no prior indication . . ."	212
Cold Front	213
Vital Matters	215
Theory	217
Bulletin	218
Best Foot	219
Mixed Feelings	220
Just Deserts	222
Mooning	224

Recipe	226
Shorts Garden	227
Incredible Vistas 2	229
Now and Then	230
Airs and Graces	231
So What!	233
Inspiration is Just a Guy Called Art	234
"If you do . . ."	236
Light	238
Testing Testing Testing	240
Talking Air	242
Hotel Zingo	243
Pact and Impact	245
"The evening is falling away sharply . . ."	246
Common Denominator	247
Here Today Here Tomorrow	249
Flying	250
Post Script	252
TRANS (1989)	255
Address	257
Double Take 1	258
Double Take 2	259
Trans	261
Revisions	263
Playback	264
Rain	274
Heroic and Hatless	281
Right to Reply	282
Alias	284
Viewpoint	287

N.B.	288
Shadow Boxing	289
A Perfect Language	290
Four Songs	291
Caption Block	295
Rural Pursuits	302
Stepping Out	309
Mutant Generation	313
Song 5 (out of sequence)	314
Song 6	315
For the Record	316
LCD Ode	318
Par Avion	320
As It Is	322
Varations on Silence and Figures in a Room	323
Ferrying	326
Warnings	328
Tongues of Light	330
THE EDGE (1993)	333
Foreword	335
"Motive connects proposition . . ."	337
"Comparisons and similarities . . ."	338
"Constant terrestrial adoration . . ."	339
"Trodden earth resists the heel of penury . . ."	340
"Tell me no name bequeath no toil . . ."	341
"Subliminal desires exploit . . ."	342
"Art probe annuls waste . . ."	343
"At the time of your departure . . ."	344
"Echoes vibrate through frowsy evening light . . ."	345
"Energy defined by the excess it harbours . . ."	346

"You were alone in your room . . ."	348
"As much about not retelling . . ."	350
"Random probes dispatched to aimless wandering . . ."	352
"Though dead and lost . . ."	353
"Sometimes music too is inadequate . . ."	354
"Many ways and many other ways . . ."	355
"Wherever you settle contradicts . . ."	356
"How you describe how it was then. . . ."	358
Coda	359

ART FOR OTHERS (1998)   361
    Art for Others   363

DELIGHT'S WRECKAGE (2001)   381
    Shining Channels   383
        Shoal   383
        Interval   384
        Dead Letter Drop   385
        Shift   386
        Revisionary   387
        The Excommunicant   388
        Recoil   389
        Invisible Detachments   390
    Where Once Was   391
        Further Instructions   391
        Moves   392
        Interrogation   393
        Thomas's Splint   394
        A Rant   395
        Ritual   396
    Passages   397
        passages   397

camouflage	398
findings	399
masque	400
ancient wishes	402
Variations	403
ancient wishes 2	403
fragment	404
incidental	406
variations	407
break	408
at warren street	409
echo	410
deep pile	411
Elsewhere in Disguise	412
commercial break	412
sub-tropical garden	414
airing	416
no name	418
song fragment	419
Marking the Blue	420
for	420
naming	422
ruse	423
repair	425
chronicle	426
Delight's Wreckage	427
nocturne	428
excursion	430
fable	432
damage field	433
cause	434

Acknowledgments

I looked at my bookshelves, my address book and copies of old magazines to obtain guidance for this note. What transpired finally touches this page. Through a curious life of varied fortune I have consistently appreciated the support of Andrew & Jean Crozier, Philip & Jane Crozier, Tim Longville, Peter Riley, Robert Vas Dias, John Hall, John Welch, Rod Mengham, Peter Hodgkinson, Ian McKelvie, Tony Frazer, the late Douglas Oliver, the late John Riley, Barry Dixon, Andrew Duncan, Nick Kimberley, Ian Patterson, John Davies, Patrick Caulfield; and in America, Michael Palmer, John Yau, Tony Towle and Rosmarie and Keith Waldrop.

Christopher and Jennifer Hamilton-Emery at Salt did what publishers should do; exercised patience, forbearing and perseverance in guiding this book to publication. My thanks to them both.

There are so many writers, poets and friends who have lived with me through this life that I suspect another volume would not do justice to them and their contribution. Needless to say they are always in my mind.

Where are we now? On the brink of the future. Never giving up. Always going on.

Uncollected Early Poems

Wish You Were Here

I've always considered that phrase
Lacks sincerity and as a generalisation
Of true feelings falls short of any mark
However I must write now
Accept its proposition
As expressing my immediate desire
A two and a half hour transatlantic conversation
Can never equate to my being
There, or you here, or both of us elsewhere,
But together
I do wish you and I were together,
Here or there.
Which is neither here nor there
Because the wish is not sufficient

LONDON / NEW YORK
1979

Tonight the glass is filled frequently
With enough alcohol to determine the immediate
Future events. Avoiding the clumsy hands
Reaching for another, drink.
Presently exposed to uncompromising doubts.
Regaining balance as the chair topples
Under me. Good morning out there.
My vision is distorted but essentially pure.
My head falls forward into stupor.
Hello sunrise, your birds are calling.
Their song is chorused by the silence
But makes little sense, finally.
Where is home this week?
I cannot see the way out of here.
The place is . . .
In the future of memory
In the recall of the coming days

circa OCTOBER 1979

white flakes peel from the wall
the apple tree grows against

sinuous limbs splay across the gutter
in a tangle of unravelled ideas

like dust in the underworld
gripping the slate pitch avidly

holding last year's wind-falls
on the slope

bright spheres outlasting the season
yellowed and pungent in their

inevitable decay
brimming with a concealed possibility

of growth as days disperse and broadcast
autumn's frequent rain

the dreamlight of embracing loss
wasp cavities collapsing to the fibrous core

dark seed withering
beneath a skin of mulch a flesh of sterile pulp

3 JANUARY 1970

Vesalii Icones
(Andreas Vesalius: De Humani Corporis Fabrica)
for Peter Maxwell Davies

a doorbell rings
at the end of the nineteenth century
whispers of a dying era
in a darkened hallway
we are listening
and the folds of brocade
redolent with tobacco smoke
fray at the touch of a hand
condemned to service
in rooms of dreams
and distorted perspective
gaslights splutter like asthmatics
the twisting flames
dance without argument
the doorbell rings
like a scream fraying

❋

hysterical syncopations dance in your blood
dreaming Nijinsky sane, his arena of success
a fabulous ballet, depraved librettist at best
a true philosopher, otherwise a rodent dictator

❋

not close enough to imagine
the energy
the music consumes

in a hotel lobby in Zurich
or was it Prague
palms flanking the doors of mahogany
where the performance affects
the lives of an audience
of strangers,
tremble and fret
in the dry mid-summer air
the fronds shadow-box
on walls of faux marble
outside limousines collect
fur and jewellery
in debauched disarray

this hysterical scene,
in which each participant
manages a role
of considerable proportion
slips into mayhem and panic,
the faces dissolve
the year drifts into an index
of months weeks days
first lines acknowledgements
and reference

✺

why do I sit here
exposed to such sententious tones

I have walked in a street
narrow as a vein
in a town possessed

whose hand manipulates
the turncoat puppet of
social deconstruction

black boots stand empty
at the door
where light falls brazen
from an addled sun
in the late occult afternoon

the slippers dance
silently in a vacant theatre

remote within my clothes
I claim the day

❋

"it is a thoroughly modernist day"
she announces
glass light cuts
her bleached hair into narrow strands

her red lips move
and mould the words she sings
a continuum in mime
each movement a gesture of incestuous delight

he does not lack desire
but dreams only the bitter kisses
on her adored body

they wander in the rancid fields
of harvest
crippled with gestures of desire

*

dawn soothes the empty rooms
he moves exquisitely
suede light on stained glass

his nakedness dazzles the walls
the mirror imitates his every action

hands shape gestures of desire
his skin shines
eyelids purple with fatigue

self-ravished and lustful
he is aching to hold

listless graceful
ravishing the silent image in the glass

24 July / 6 August 1970

I cannot move
buds throb outside the window

letters arrive
stained with adventure
the ghosts of foreign tongues
gummed under each flap

wandering words accumulate
stagger off the page
in festival bewilderment

it is not freedom
merely a form of verbal breakdown
corrupting purpose

luminous blue smoke plumes
in the ruffled air
above crippled chimneys

a scrambled alphabet
on the explicit sky

I remember northern lights
the united states of america
is struggling to conquer
the scorched star of asia

it is spring in the trees

28 APRIL 1970

disappearance is rendered more terrible   for being so complete
the longing   broken ornaments of regret   fill the haunted rooms

whatever displacement restores past intimacy lacks the shapeliness
of the heroine's presence in this day   and the manifestation
beyond the sentinel rushes   on the sparkle and flash of the water's surface
the lake reaching towards you   grass fringe   banks of red earth
a place with which you are not familiar   curse of brilliance and unforgiving
      blue

ah miss jessel   your ghost   and dark mysterious acts
thrill and entice me   an arm placed across my shoulder   a hand in my hand
a mouth across my lips

the lake shore   the house and formal gardens   eroticism by the influence
of your movements   electric desire   self continuation through the elastic
strata of your sensuality   lost soul in the pliable substance that surrounds us

connect to the day in moments of charged precision   between the act
and the intention   between your loss and this desire

5 FEBRUARY 1971

Going Out For Cigarettes

mid august ennui haunted by
mid september cool

betrayed 4 days ago
in the morning sunlight
pushing out long shadows
on fields grey with moisture

& tonight
going out for cigarettes from
the machine without my jacket
a sharp chill catches under my shirt
like a shoal of small silver fish
aerating the night tide

the luminous halo
from a bisected moon
behind shallow drifts of cloud
reflects off damp rooftops

& the small stars
complete their journey of light years
duration in the moment
my pupils locate them
and the day slides off inevitably & dark

14 AUGUST 1970

Poem for Mary

(stepping from shade):

    in abrupt sunlight
she adores the faultless sky,
body of burnished gold :

        her face,
charmed concern , bedecked &
flowing with darkly velvet hair:
    eyes acute satin :
intense lips , a pleated cushion
    sewn with flowers :

the breath   the breath inspires:
    drunken nobility rampage at the door,
      not to be ignored   :
    weeds simper a brief invocation:
my body pays homage to your pristine
ministrations

circa **1970**

a quick gesture attracts my attention

        the meaning of you
    to remind also of your presence

                (& lack)

        for the hand lies
    empty
            touching air
& the scent of you lingers

      vaguely persisting

circa 1970

The Photographs

you turn and blur badly
all those people that so much has altered
and so little changed in the face of propaganda
'field' 'tree' 'sky' 'cloud' 'bird' 'hill' 'ruin'
various dates   the ink fades   the strangers
particularly Albert, smiling and benign, one foot
on the gate   of 1931
clumsy bi-planes in sepia hangars
laughing at the new unnaturalness
pressing the shutter   guessing the image
living in the ballast of blank spaces
all these occasions
and the preoccupation with postcards
backwards into the future   turning the pages
seeing the lives there

6 APRIL 1971

because you are
by chance by destiny by all
manner of fateful accident decree
or otherwise

beside me
naked
within the loop
of my arms

I wld say to you only
                my love
this time is ours by chance by
destiny or otherwise
by fine calculation of unknowns
& quantities & qualities to an
nth degree or
otherwise
        & love sits at my right
hand & at my left sits
love or otherwise
            I wld say little else
            I wld say perhaps not this
wld move with the artistry of
deft embrace

(enfold you
 to slow climax)

or otherwise

circa 1970

this place

    a dream
        of inconstancy

   sheets of billowing wind
mismanage our hair

        coarse grasses yield
previously untrodden
                beneath our feet

I would ask no more than such as this remain
        unfettered
& grasses grow
                free as emotion
      & stones
lie altered
      by no man

                            LATE 60'S

```
leaning over
      the mean
   pencil scribblings
              a lamp burns
behind my hand
                dispersing
      the room's clutter of
                   belongings
             into a distant
darkness
       no longer
    behind my crouched figure
but further
      in a mysterious place

      strange
           devoid of personal
                feeling

   surprising then      from that

                this poem
```

                                    1966

you do not believe in the definition of a wall

overgrown with pressed flowers
ornamental relatives
and rectangular memories

you are wary of stairs
with their brief and disconcerting levels
that dare the effortless push
towards a smouldering point
where horizontal forces converge
and hysterical distortions deflate
the armchair and the painted screen
and spongy panic that contracts

a gloved and elegant hand passing the pill
of sugar-coated illusions

20 December 1971

let us say that by his presence he intimidates
those abt him
who in turn calculate for themselves
various attitudes to act
as diversions to his violence   he is shouting
let us propose that his purpose is to cleave
a passage through the pliable air
pushing his bicycle the while
with determination   unable to accept
or comply
     with the morning's attitude
                incomprehensible words
phrases repeated again and again   directed at
the pavement, the mean sky, the pliant bicycle,
the crowd jeering behind
expressionless eyes,
         demons
he dribbles
     saliva and foam speckle his jaw and shirt front
                        we
are assailed by his private anger
          let us assume his purpose is some form of ease
let us consequently speculate
and reach the conclusion that
                        he is incomplete
to us
   but to himself and his many selves not so
                    awaiting the loaded silence

20 MARCH 1969

he adapts to the inertia in the room
becomes his own ghost
haunting forced confinement
the walls are powdery
his arm reaches through the open window
he is vindicated
and the line reaches a point in his imagination years later
before he has acknowledged it in new time
desperately he moves from   illusions of permanence
strain becomes excessive
certain moments of obtuse significance disappear
certain interference from long ago becomes sometime soon
you speak to him   you are not there

                                                 3 MARCH 1971

there are times
you simply lean
towards me
slip your arm
around my shoulder
& kiss me

there are times
you are surprised
by my cunning

there are times
neither of us
says a single
        word

                    1967

dark pages   slow turns   brief salves (1969)

1

it is

    a landscape

  I cannot explain

       the colours
      assail my
         eyes

     I am dizzy
with purity
    lack of pollution

   the full fields
        mad
   with wheat

           & I
    watch the
sprung seed
    jealously

2

& love you

```
the day slips
the white chairs crouch
            the lawn folds onto itself
    the leaves exude a darkness
the day is given no title
            rain has closed in
surrounding all who are naked to it
            the bastions of
support
        deteriorate
decay hangs in the air
                        I have
        named it &
        admit to its existence
the 4 winds rampage
the white chairs
            leap
```

star gazer
    upholder of myth
    author of choice adventures
        iconoclast of dreams
watch them edge away
        absurdly dubious
    as you roll on the ground
in paroxysms of laughter
    hands clasped across the
        narrow belly of
    your insanity

I speak of one
who will not
acknowledge even
my glance (that
which is a page of
my heart's book)
do I therefore allow
that a smile would be an
impertinence

                        you are
not part of this company
                I seek your
rare laughter
            delicate hand to
slip mine   a captured
bird pursuing freedom

elusive glance to relinquish
its economy
                I fear the invidious
clock
        the uncharitable hour

& query the road
            which makes
travellers of us all

so we watch him totter,
filthy , clubfooted ,
crouched beneath a
small pack
    & weight of years

watch him hobble
    towards evening &
   the morning star hostel;
      both a certain
destination
   to one of
 arbitrary movements

that speech gags the mouth & words sleep
lightly on the page   (what matter
that windows reflect a passing moon offers
only a factor of the night's motion

fields reel at the topsyturvy tread of sly
dreams   the sight is duped by phantasmagoria

that page   that window   they are alive
a clock bangs against a wall   a dark page
slowly turns

     not simply this
         or that decision
     of discontinuance
             nor the inclination
       towards future
                 enigmatic
           recollections
     but the dull chastening
                 fact
           of oblivion

take

the light from
the intensity
of her face

though carefully

knowing the
    delicate
  movements
              &
being silent
     so hear
the
    shudder of
escaping
       breath

              such gleanings
in the space
           between the
     regarding
                  engraved
across this
            short distance
     which is a
            remoteness
I offer discreet comment –
this as a token of my
response

delicately
         Spring free
sprung free
           the bud
   folds
        /back its
brown husk
          revealing—

as
  the hymen   opens
             for
     first love

                        not that
the act becomes simple
        a commonplace
a routine
            but that its necessity
    involves a process
                        to be reckoned
            with
                    a continuance of
the initial problem
                extended into (towards)
vast calculations

lady
whose raven hair whose fruitful lips
whose breasts of swans down whose
hands of confirmed promise whose body of
strange infliction
                    smiles at me in slow
motion
        I wish I had Argus eyes therewith
to gaze in fabulous content

horde

give rapt attention to the strident song
                          born of
remote
gesture
              hither by
              some
              divine
              indecency

an exorcism
    (of sorts)
a putting into place
writing down
         a rearrangement
         of said things

there is a calculated
         objectivism

a notion of final assembly

the folds
of your
rumoured
dress
    wheeze
in my fingers,

        such simplicity
        there,
          what more
        to say ?

        summer,

bees grumble on
the dog-rose

Gift

couldn't I
    employing such composure
with delightful gesture
& surprisingly
      place this offered kiss
          onto your
mouth
  so slightly open
in mock
      amazement

awake to your savagery as you rent the turf's
structure   cut the sandy earth & roll pebbles
white as a virgin's thighs   over & over along
slender wayward channels in mud-foamy waters
storm rain gutting the impressionable ground

                                        slithers

the window
just open

              rain
the coolness
of it
    through the
    aperture
         touching
    my face

is it you
       my love

the elderberries turn
from green
      to deepest
   purple

oyster-catchers throng the striated shore
    shingle rinsed with supine waves
sighs forward & back   hauled by the
scrounging tide
          out in the bay red sailed
yachts dip on the buckled swell
leaning from the breeze   marsh grasses
hiss along the silted estuary where a boy
spins flat stones over ripples

        the birds
            break suddenly
    into air

do we speak of the metaphor
implied by this strewn path,
gold/ ochre/ & those many colours

; or let be what is   ,wise
to the natural process   , regard
less of words struggling to clarity:

this
    , the last day of october
                     , all is
                            said

we make the silence

to come

        rooms strain
        to our
        presence

    the furniture identifies
  our pressure

we make
the silences
to come
      our voices dismiss
      the solemn
      stillness

          the moments
          slip by through
          the dark hours

the distances spread between us

& the rain falls
      slack as string

journeys wld be the measure
they had told me
              of yr experience

so I have moved

        (though with some
trepidation)

          confining myself
to territory of known quality
to explore all the avenues
the possibilities

        now I think to
    travel elsewhere
      having seen so little
  of my destinations

usually it's early morning
when I see him walking

        a figure direct
        from
        Lowry's
        Salford
   the boots
   mackintosh
   shoulders
      head pushed
      into the
      wind
hands lost in
      frayed pockets
         spacious & derelict
       eyes enduring a
       temporary freedom
 & birds mocking
  in all innocence
the lanes a clamour of twittering

     he recedes in distance
     thrown back as a face
     in harsh laughter
simple as the wind he voyages
        placid in the day's havoc

wld say it thus

a dark cumulus / strata of
cloud
       the fullmoon
       hung as from this (that is
   placed below
           the cloud's
                consistence

, & gone

or,
      moonlight of that wild colour
      of pale ,
          disturbing the earth,
   defines (half-tones)   , spills shadows

            peels each ripple
            from the stream

further
     , (moon's dependence on
     atmospheric condition),

             that is:
cloud / no moon
no moon / cloud

      (interchange of each)
   & their dependence on the other

       (as we depend upon a
       presence
           & conversely

upon an absence

       for we are marked by
       such conditions

            which form
           a part
of how our souls move

so it wld

the moon rises full
seen into cloud   is gone

rooks from the trees black as the
far end of night
          lifting above the branch tips
          settling on sparse stubble
under the crumbling sky
the first star visible through a web of
pines   dark along the skyline
a vociferous flock of crows   tumultuous
          in the evenings timorous clarity
slanting   angled out of sight
                    the throbbing
call of wood-pigeons fading to silence

dusk
          a shrewd owl swooping
          from tree to tree
          its laconic call rejoicing
          the night

the wild duck
flies over the
flat river
pastures , directly

       into the sun
       set:
       cows stoop,
       drink at
shallows,

each ripple
mouths the
stones , plucks
       the reeds,

       constantly

the heron creaks low,

stuttering to
a mono
stance
in the marsh
pool:
       times
       mutations
continue ,

I am alien
to the field's
width;
       the scarecrow,
       travesty of
       man ,

is more a part,

arms out
spread , as if
that lordly gesture ,

I own from here
        to here

whispered from
the warped
lips
        silent as
the merest breeze
in grass
        as the
        feet of
        the peewit
landing on
stubble

    broken line traces out condition,
        we see it as fragmented statement ,
        removed from context

                the fruits ferment,
              you wander in the reeking
                    orchard , I , also

      as if expecting a return of eagles
        you scan the low clouds   , gorse aflame
with flowers
      , the broken fence along the
      quarries ragged lip
            , posts punched into the porous
        sandstone,
        leaning out
        to vacant spaces

for David Sims

our voices echo , for want of
the ordered articles that absorb
sound ,   herde the resonant
utterings

the dust of dispersed paraphernalia
seethes in the hollow room
                ,you take your last
                look round , & close
                the door on its
                settling,
clatter down the melancholy stair
into afternoon sunlight

at once   accepting the brief salves
& regretting a move
                        so decisive

against wall

    takes   spillage off gutters
    the temporary fusions
    of light

        such conditions

    the effete nature of the day
    tensions constriction
                disregarded

    (walls scoured face wrenched
     to fragments by the yellow
     bulldozer
            light flipped
            through to
    soak the drawling shadows

a child stamps its foot
nanny turns disturbed eyes
a hand is raised
a window shut
                      trees reflect
                      in puddles
piano lesson

trembling   fingers lean to
touch
pain

intricate as
a single note   hung in
october afternoon haze

    what "time" could dispel

                              this eternal
                                                motion
                containing as it does
                          the meditative
  qualities of euphoria

                      to exist suspended
                      between the imagination
                      and the memory

                      vacant of those qualities
  assuming a position in the natural

                            refinements of
                            daily commerce

          at once involved
                  & free

                            treading the
                            narrow line
  through the
          vacuum & continuum

A Personal Poem
for John Hall

    1

to investigate the day allows so many
"aspects" for embrace   I had
thought   this morning   the sun now
really betrayed time   (the season)
with various qualities of illumination
    light falling on   & revealing the
used worn colours

so I come to the present   sitting on this
window sill   the sun shining through glass
onto my back   reading "Between The Cities"
& hearing beyond my voice
the stillness of autumn's beginnings   (a yawn
in warm sunlight)
                          & the words sing
of things more vast than world & time
& relationship   I wonder abt some hidden
nostalgia not known directly to me   or
some vehicle perhaps of my own imaginative
desires   exposed by the "framing of questions"

            2

      the sea moves close
      to where you live
      in these days
      exposing the water's
      girth between
      continents

    & I cannot help but
muse over what
occupies you   at this
moment   as I read
these words

                             & occasional leaves
                                  fall
                                        & drift
                  making change a
                  known quantity

moving   round you   the sun   its axis   the sun
's light   insisting   trees fringing the hard line
against air   the ridge   branches   feathered out
towards a perfection of form   the order & intention
of trees   their leaves a debris of bright
copper-shards   gathering against obstruction
becoming   by degrees   limp with moisture   flattened
the shape beaten   lost as leaf mould   a
return to organic matter

        out   at the edge

  hard blue merging into   extremes of neutral/
            that grey
preying on sight/refracting the lights run

evening liquid a decanting of hours
the extemporary gesture
      a progression

motion   day   as aspect   infinite
the trembling differences of light/
       to light

we make of this complex   a simple acceptance
clarify our desires   programme our intentions

move into landscapes/winding darkness/the mute
stone   statuesque/compelling
       the moon edges from
all this   piercing the sky like that moment   in the act
of love
  & the progression (as mentioned) turns turns turns

so you see there in all her cool glory   the moon
                                  not the sun   the moon
& the orbit   the route of *her* intended course

                from which we (can) draw parallels
shd we choose
                        as the sun also
                        as we
                        seek a form
                        of conclusion

Sunlight

appears on
      , breaks,
           down the wall
's vertical surface   .
              moved/adjusted
              by texture's
          , projection here ,

recess else
where

           from
           this day's shrouded
           sky , (october chill
           banished to a merest
           suggestion of cold),
           this sudden movement
           of light ,

falling to where   colours
appeal for attention

    did I say from here we can hear
    trains   the swish of lorries one
    road away   spasmodic voices cleaving
    the night
                our speech
                    a cross-reference
            codification of events we
                        destroy with words
            a necessary conflict

            as the poem
            becomes the precise act
        of volition
                    an obligation
        structure which takes the voice to
                            speech with
                words for the lady / &
        the location

Year of Meteors (1972)

Five hours of darkness fill the window
you don't usually count hours
but tonight they seem more seriously intent
on passing
in awe of the paraphernalia
you sleep
overtake the conflict
spaced out somewhere north of Leeds

standing by the double doors
the voice fails
its parabolic curve dipping into linoleum
briefly you consider the span
concentration climbs through the ruin
pushing a foundation stone aside

14 JANUARY 1971

Breakfast

at 7.45 the door opens
I dress my hunger
and greet the unsteady breakfast room
clockwork waiters assault the wax mannequins
crumbs of sleepy toast float in the coffee
the languid ceremony continues without consequence
high and indistinct the ceiling is ignored
newspapers describe bizarre events
and fragile opinions
chairs fold back displacing crushed napkins
skilful hands restore order
confidence is arranged on the glass shelf with
peppermint toothpaste and a comb

17 JANUARY 1971

Twice

fresh bread and a smile
there is always the unexpected
proving density of presence exists
her charms sail proudly the waves of my scrutiny
crimson lips stain the edge
of the facial expression
a lazy smile again   nudging her cheeks
questions line up at the margin
well lubricated machinery carries the situation
to a conclusion of words
she mentions the angularity of music
the slippery distortion of breathing
the dilemma of a current response
the excellence of anticipation

2 FEBRUARY 1971

voices flap deviously
the wireless crackles
in heavy darkness the workrooms sparkle
glass beads fall from a snapped string
cascade and clatter in heavy darkness
scatter across the estuary
further south a settlement has been established
the cupboard contains old clothes
set aside for the winter season
moisture saturates the air
and our perfunctory conversation
becomes visible

3 FEBRUARY 1971

The Hotel Temporary

an ambitious conversation in the adjoining room
the laughter of someone's joy
sudden wind furling the gothic curtains
his sneezes continued throughout the night
and few of the guests were able to sleep
until after his early departure

the green telephone a symbol to those
expecting a message
their nervous anticipation displaced along the corridors
in and out of the bars and of the day
without a name it was impossible to seek contact
one of us was going to have to make a move
sooner or later
without a name
and of course when everyone was absorbed
by the latest bulletin   and least expecting it
the door closed   thud

3 FEBRUARY 1971

"nor forget I to sing the wonder"
Year of Meteors / Robert Indiana / 1961

eventually the track widened
and he was able to walk beside his companion

in the journal such information
had been recorded
the structure and dimensions of escarpments
and mineral deposits in river-beds

always conscious of the nocturnal performance
of stars   and galaxy patterns
they improvise a canvas chart accurately
inscribed with the positions of mysterious
and autonomous systems
it came to be known as 'the big ceiling'

the calendar of the expedition was renamed
Year of Meteors   in honour

4 FEBRUARY 1971

broken ornaments
regrets and yearning haunt the house
a terrible absence abused by memories

whatever displacement heals
the rift   lacks the shapeliness of the heroine's
presence   blurred form reaching from a place
you are not familiar with

Miss Jessel ! Your name surrounds me
you impress your will subvert my desires
I greet your ghost to copulate in empty rooms
potent with your determination
and influence
my illness is merely exhaustion
your pliable and erotic body drips about me
as I spill into you for the last and first time

abandoning the lesson of house and lawn
for the continuous transgression of your lake bed
where I piss on the spiky rushes of contrition
for your joy

5 FEBRUARY 1972

you walk through the door and a year passes
tonight I had decided on several definitions
of genius but was able to destroy the evidence
this seems always the surest approach to
total awareness   thank you   your timely arrival
was particularly appreciated
the entire evening has been somewhat strained
and analytical
trying to remember the uncomplicated sunlight
of the day I realised I could not swim and the sea
would not accept my thrashing
retaliation was unsuccessful
my anxiety a slow destruction of the problem
spread thickly with morbid cigarettes
making tea and exchanging news and anecdotes
rectifies the situation with a soothing sense of
understatement

6 FEBRUARY 1971

it becomes a monday morning inside the clock
inside the room
I have cleaned my teeth and removed my shirt
in preparation   but cannot quite decide
that to retire to bed is the right thing

muffled shouts assume a tone of shiftless
and uneasy antiquity
stiff joints work slowly back to elastic
agility and contort to all those beautiful
shapes we admire in the paintings

what friends are doing remains a secret
it is difficult to fix their whereabouts with
any degree of accuracy

beset with international airmail I look from
the letter disturbed by the question of location
clearly we were mistaken about the number of
correspondents
it is not clear what the next move
might be

7 February 1971

    an incoming tide
                  sand darkens accordingly
    they are running   the air falls apart
                             as they force
    an oblique cascade

                 glitter , he shouts , and
    good morning
               as they jump down the steps
    both know exactly who the stranger is

                          from then to
    the poem   imagine two years of memorable living
    the schooner sails close inshore
    a landing party rows backwards and forwards
    over the lost treasure

                                    8 FEBRUARY 1971

fatigue creeps closer under the awning
a grey landscape describes nothing
that is not also provocative when exposed
the grim visage of understatement
does not eliminate the implicit sense of
continuity   one thing merges into the next
and the differences escape interpretation

                              9 FEBRUARY 1971

Chocolate Sauce (1973)

a pattern emerges
the remote idea of having been there
continually forfeiting a position
at the banquet of massive proposals
is as if seen through a translucent screen
the background we avoid dissolves
and the idea is launched into fluency
as we side-step rising gusts of aversion
and tiny particles of doubt
with a giddy aplomb

David Chaloner.
April 1973

Swirl

wind sweeps through the tall grass at great speed like a
low flying aeroplane   the hiss of its motors is
white sound   & hollow

episode 2 encroaches on the previous line
it having been in the process of revision when the dead
line arrived

a time allowance has not been established
certain excuses suffice to ensure ease of continuity
often at the expense of integrity
assuming integrity exists   and is not a fictional
affectation

(pause)

returns stealthily through the trees the lake frowns
gathered pleats pushed to the far shore
yes   you've guessed it   the wind's returned

slack telephone wires lift & spread   horizontal arcs
from pole to pole
leaves get up   swirl   tying lovely knots in the wind

13 FEBRUARY 1971

sunlight slants in through the window
clouds are heaped together
                        travelling so that
  they obliterate and emphasise
                           the blue
I have little appetite
preferring to drink coffee
and read a book of poems
to which I am not giving
my fullest attention

nothing seems very concise today
what is present
is a network
        of variations
the vague and lethal stillness
                          reveals
a recently discovered
        lack of reality
    in all its chill and eventless glory

                              15 FEBRUARY 1971

the problem the grass under the saplings
the form the adaptable
grid structure the depth the russian
salad the present whereabouts the point
of entry the relative the termination
the working range the yet to be established
the master of assemblies
the loose and public afternoon the regarding
colour the paint will turn the edges
of the idea
the geometric disturbances the optical
trickery that exists the design
a hinge facilitates the altered
direction and angle the nervously
aware the problems extend to shake the glass
of water placed below the panel
the problems lounge about miserably like a wet morning
waiting for the sudden jolt or spongy push
and the lines go right on by them
sparkling with success
towards the charming innocence of a wall

1/2 MARCH 1971

he is exploring the inertia of the room
which is transitional   & quickly concedes
to the moving figure   he is his own ghost
we admire & chastise his habit of interpretation

the walls are powdery   he stretches
his arm out   towards the
through the open window

bored desperate he moves away from illusions
of permanence
with the tentative steps of a novice high-wire walker
reckless concentration is the means by which
he achieves insularity

segments of a personal timetable chip away
strain is excessive
certain moments impossible

you speak to him   you are not there

3 MARCH 1971

move

through tinted glass a man a chair two men a
desk a man   papers and files the time is between
morning and evening a day of the week a blue
van awaits who are on the move very seriously
fifteen houses in a short time folded close to the
threadbare gardens demolition the green hoardings
ablaze torn posters metaphorical flames
catch the bus let it go it was easy Mr Coleridge
this is what you were at writing Kubla Khan
strange is conception is outcome is mobility spirit
assonance the window open and the day a slightly
unyielding colour opium dreams lakes
rivers to a sunless sea strewn with rubble the air
rises falls sweet honey-dew
the blue van drives away

1 April 1971

to go adrift seemingly given extra time   to receive
false information   a known hazard   disguised
as personal opinion becomes dogma
lacks distinction and substance
                              enough to fail
to escape a meaningless exchange
                                concentration
is feigned   the man is at the edge of days
strewn with pitfalls and stumbling blocks

the view is injected with a gasp of surprise
                                    a vertical
stress of upwards   he turns around
     loses his place   remembers to launch a smile
it's that easy   the prompt anticipation

                                        1 April 1971

Itch

    in the hay barn
           beneath tilt of trees
leaning off bracken scrolled slopes

rough edge of cloud stacked
on the horizon

see through access
at high level   hay on the hills
clouds acting like a sliding door

ladder angled off the edge of the loft
dusty light propped on the back wall
for making shadows for watching time
for leaping over
           right back into the
   itchy darkness

                              1 APRIL 1971

The Situation

we have lost our sense of ease and are gaining
a tact that is almost becoming

they employ restraint against the trick of illusion
releasing "it wasn't meant to end this way" and
"the entire situation has become odious"

we are quite calm and working well within our limits
which have no distinction   there is much to be done
and although we don't know where we are we make a place

4 APRIL 1971

The Photographs

you turn and blur badly
all those people that so much has altered
and so little changed in the face of propaganda
'field' 'tree' 'sky' 'cloud' 'bird' 'hill' 'ruin'
various dates   the ink fades   the strangers
particularly Albert, smiling and benign, one foot
on the gate   of 1931
clumsy bi-planes in sepia hangars
laughing at the new unnaturalness
pressing the shutter   guessing the image
living in the ballast of blank spaces
all these occasions
and the preoccupation with postcards
backwards into the future   turning the pages
seeing the lives there

6 April 1971

Domestic Scenes

a brush climbs the stairs
the dusty leap admires the sweeping motion

thursday hots up
things happen and are accomplished totally

the telephone will open a space between
our voices despite the grey of the sky
that has suddenly and without warning
or consideration become the blue of the sky

there is no one home to answer
the adroit shouldering of the lateness
of the afternoon at the door the bottom step
and on up

9 APRIL 1971

    a landslide carries the background from sight
the profile of the journey
is set down gingerly alongside
    the sparsely annotated impression gathered previously
the most open of eyes cast obliquely
as a fleeting moment on the timetable   recounts
    and has you looking up   he sniffs   likes the way
it works   the clarification
his ardour and brisk stylish panache
    bending cutting and gluing the cardboard scenery
for the systematic fabrication of a landscape
where we will settle down to solve the logical
    sequence of all that is imposed
on the pattern of so much we have yet to
fully understand
    the openings are within our range
by the time we are prepared and aware that
to go back to our former selves is to remain
    and to advance is to accept what is offered
and the chance to rework destiny with clear-headed
abstraction   our responsibilities variously defined
    we take our differing ways
providing extensions that will later form mere fragments
of a definitive vacillation
    rendering the ensuing happiness unique and misunderstood

                                          14 April 1971

Racers

another dragged necklace sliding to meet
its spring-loaded catch
the name is on the tickets lying snugly in the pockets
of glum passengers
a closed level-crossing signals and the brakes are held
having seen the leaders they cheer from opened windows
their shirts of startling colour and design
speed falls murderously across their breath accelerating
from gates where the leaders lost their advantage
clicking gears cope with a whizzing terrain
the fast miles determine a forgiving conclusion
of co-ordinates sliced firmly between the pressures of speed

16 April 1971

Exercise

chocolate sauce on ice-cream
coffee and an appraisal of intentions

the wind chews away at us
we face it bravely and it warms us

the ice-cream loses zero
as we walk towards oxford circus

the chocolate and the coffee mingle
happily along the digestive tracts

❋

the rain nibbles at the puddles
the new leaves bite the spring air

the spring air contains some element
that flicks open the covers of the new leaves

blossoms laughingly expose their charms
and enthralled showers get dashed to the ground

23 APRIL 1971

not merely false starts
the frequent collision of basic presumptions
but the great biblical deluge
prophetic and retrospective conversation

the false starts
the static elements that surround the encounter
anonymous and not to be remembered
we remember them
the language unravels like string from
a brown paper parcel

the paper is folded open to reveal
the room
in which we sit
dealing with the process of communication

misdirected we stumble through the ornamental
maze   attempting to regain our orientation
and composure we use the string as a guide line
until its length is exhausted

the flase starts   the regrets   the desire
for subsequent amendments

24 APRIL 1971

Texture

lines of colour across the table
salvaged morning
it could have rained it didn't
relief?   I'm unsure
space opening out inside here

the room is quietly
bursting

         24 APRIL 1971

the patrons sip their drinks
posing professionally under

the spot lights   bereft of
purpose   the colours you have chosen

blue and the green of your search
at speed the inclement weather

the conversations lack continuity
are less impressive than the sky

a sliding lid of rain
rises diagonally from the painting

so that the smudged musicians are
by the river   on the wall

are the subject of a raucous voice
bubbles unable to contain the coast

of north africa   the beautiful daughter
or the cargo

that we might unload deep inside
her   rising diagonally

to a point forty miles further on

25 MAY 1971

as we drive back today   from yesterday
it is the next morning we're travelling
along the edge of   the softly expanding dawn
parallel with the darkness
not to prevent its withdrawal
or the loss of some quality
that has been endearing to us
rather   to detain the multifarious thrill
of advancing light
that disarmingly enacts its furtherance
around our direction

                                                                   31 MAY 1971

surf falls noisily along the tunnel of half-closed
eyes   a weight of stones and fuzzy warmth adds to
the discomfort   the one presses gently against the
other close to the fluttering silk panels that play
tricks with the light
further along the coast a red bathing cap encourages
inaccuracy   waves smash down on its cavorting
the jaunty swimmer rises from the water exhausted
steps back into the puzzling construction of habit
that encloses him in its tailored sleeve
such vivid encounters continue to deflect the pressure
that pills erode with the art of their chemistry
and the fragments of a brittle day's discomfort
fuse with compensatory tones

4 JUNE 1971

recently having returned from a long journey
he delights in relating the events of his stupendous
departure   the narrative is far-fetched and
deliberately complex   with the aim of bestowing

dignity and some plausible logic to the anecdote
the confrontation is violent   colours and slow
motion   forlorn splintering   changeling voices fail
to detail a sense of objectivity

the event crashes sideways   a shout crumbles dusty
spectators under the dried biscuit sun
the vertical emphasis fails totally to diminish the
extreme acts of sensationalism

his self-conscious act is fraught with righteous striving
refulgence stuns the saturated day

17 JUNE 1971

and the nets hung on
timber posts
sometimes it is the hand
an outspread hand
and the sky-divers

come to touch our reveries
and all the movements
not preceded by a question
rings and bracelets in the drawer

the river bank   painted primary colours
the fabulous midsummer bulk
of a forgotten lover
agitates the hardened answers

the taut mooring ropes
a tide going in and out behind his ear
the small boats there
and all the speculative devices

17 JUNE 1971

    your arrival is delayed in the public address system
as jets roar off into lacy air
    announcements from revised air-waves congest
the main terminal building
    crouched in a palm of sonic activity
the date and the fine weather contrive to give some credibility
    to the month of june
supplying glossy episodes of temperate days seems quite natural
    suddenly   and the sun glints boldly
from the glass walls of the control building
    in the sky instructions are translated with sparkling logic
the pace   becomes self-generating
    baggage glides from hand to fuselage
with uncanny precision
    sensible declarations continue to inform passengers
whose conversations touch me with a certain awe
    who are transformed
to a state of aerial perception
    that excludes my casual waiting
and you arrive six hours later by train
    your words bearing the faded shadows of altitude

                            20 JUNE 1971

instinctively advances towards adventure
calculating the terminal experience
on an immense excitement graph
that folds away into any ample pocket stitched cunningly
to the indispensable raincoat purchased specifically
for the purpose

maps are too vague he concludes
heading across country for the several answers
his departure relieves a considerable pressure
established during the argument about the darker areas
and the problem of translation

some of the less experienced explorers return to the
cities and fabricate positions of respect
become celebrities and move from one awe-struck gathering
to the next

he is reported to have said; we were nowhere
off balance   obscure   weary from the pressures of air
and responsibility of our discoveries

the fires burn brightly and cast huge forms on the
sloping tents   he makes an entry in his log-book
that is later to reveal his genius

20 JUNE 1971

Visiting

the room is at the rear of the building
we are directed there along corridors of fussy anticipation
disturbed by absences
and sticky moments of loneliness

the science of exhaustion   a fragile conversation shatters
the remote privacy
we are sitting by the window observing the sun
fabulously appear above the copse of beaches
beyond the crumbling terrace and mossy lawns

we enter the room wearing the dramatic make-up of a night's
travelling   they call a taxi to take us to the station
and we watch them depart with a flourish of loose white gravel
thrown onto the steps by spinning wheels

22 JULY 1971

The Cast in Order of Appearance

the words interlock
   a mirror gathers them together serenely
he turns and smiles as I fold back the sheets
   she sits on the edge of the unmade bed
marooned
   her language of the big break returns years later
in a fur coat
   smoking french cigarettes
posing by the door
   telling us how boring the whole scene is
the spotlight sweeps away from her face
   as the curtains swoop
maliciously
   they are unable to reach you
she straightens her dress bending towards me
   to wipe a smudge of lipstick
from the corner of my mouth
   I arrive with the bacon sandwiches
and find you sprawled in the chair
   striking flamboyant lines through the script
I can see where chalk marks have been
   hastily rubbed from the floor
they are exchanging opinions on the rehearsal
   and have missed their cue
it seems quite proper and you dash forward
   with hearty congratulations

                               22 JULY 1971

hard trees shake furtively
in the clammy sky
mouths full of enervating fluids
the humid break
the battered piano performs
with its silver wires
scorched leaves crackle into flames
and move over the dry ground
which is just one of the many signs
as the tones are indicative of
declarations and neon words burst
over the city
and the restless list of names
repairs the damage
of ill-considered words
a dense substance gathered in the sky
and the visitors arrived
and later departed

1 AUGUST 1971

Coda

peculiar dreams electrify the dormitory   we were not present
the stories percolate through a layer of time and anecdotes
the energy of the stray contact

sometimes to not know makes the right thing sensational

at the appointed time he left us   hauling the cardboard suitcase
waving his free hand   the door swung into action
the obliterated gesture   the departure recedes
there is not enough time   getting out   and quickly

from nowhere   the knife rips off a series of crude incisions
like the pen of a violent correspondent   (perhaps that should be
"the pen of a violent correspondent rips off a series of crude
incisions")

a lethal violence   the failure is one of misapplied energy
and schizoid rehearsals for notorious living   later to embellish
the portrait of genius

having premonitions seemed only a part of the newly acquired skill
taking each clue   the motives strode off in all directions

the illuminating discoveries of bizarre observers
present a compelling and stimulating document
the dormitory continues to represent a swift blow to bewilderment
its influence pressing a soft urge towards us

         22 AUGUST 1971

Dilemma

what happens above the city is a fine shuffling
the day becomes that much more than a stifling room
where haggling voices smear the air with rabid determination
if you were here I would invite you to observe the elastic
clouds   but generosity is an impossible word
and can only be liberated by the act   and truth rampages
across all this demanding honesty
a messenger will reach you soon bearing this information
no reply is expected

23 August 1971

Doors

held open by a small wedge pushed between
the lower edge and the floor

when you leave it presses against you
unwilling to allow the passage you intend
until your monster hand exerts a specific
force and respect for your urgency
takes it the other way

contrary to accepted political notions
not being a barrier is an important function
in the life of a door

numerous sensations are available
relief   the footsteps reversed
foreboding   a block of darkness standing
in the porch
delight   a company of smiling strangers
apprehension   the reversed relief of footsteps
a question answered with a question
the keyhole of the sky the lock and bolt
of a waving hand

                              25 AUGUST 1971

undisclosed destinations lurk in benzedrine timetables
the story implies that not all the secret agents returned

the reasons are deciphered and aggravate the censor
his ordinance is the sound of tearing and falling masonry

expanding into whimsical air   the spokesman for the opposition
contrary to expectations appeals to the pedestrian majority

and a ludicrous astonishment settles indelibly on the faces
of the assembled multitude   the time of proclamations

is upon us with the light-heartedness of a disposable afternoon
other versions of equally indiscriminate legislations

pour from his pen flooding the official note-paper with
vindicitive memoranda   was this then the meaning of the

revolution   our dream of a quiet and efficient dismantling
this insidious replacement from the thin files of your venom

26 August 1971

the ramp gives us a new idea
of how the elevated footpath contributes enormous vistas
to the accepted principles of scale and perspective
we walk its length, slowly ascending
rising out of ourselves to some higher point of wonder
entering with fresh news of the gradients

in these places a freshly kindled sunlight flattens
itself as rippling sails of voyages taken thankfully
across pitching oceans of spacial assiduousness
the focal point is an unfamiliar room where the primary colours
live silently, pressed against the wall
it is the brightly decorated box I will eventually give you

what we are doing is not in accordance with the official
texts and we confront their values with what we now know
the previous reality, firmly entrenched in a desire
for tangibles, that were the expression of a feverish circumscription
of the main topic, was born of an antique trepidation
which we happily commit to the museum of wild december days

16 December 1971

the notes tell of earlier occasions
spent in the diving-bell
   a continuous line terminates
behind us
        as an open situation
  we cannot avoid
other than to escape the system's glittering
enigmas

much that has become extraneous
                       lies furtively
on the table lists combine to establish
explanations both necessary and quite without
meaning
        composed from various sources
   the new set of rules disturbs
those waiting for the wrong event to move
lightly across the screen of possible
achievements

grave messages recall the wanderer
to a collision course with the days to come

                                  16 DECEMBER 1971

The Swimming-Pool Saga

    finely sewn into a tapestry of metaphysical possibilities
the footpath hurried through shrubbery and
    sensitive aromas
a bee disturbs the blossoms loaded with a cargo of yellow pollen
    hands and voices shape the later days of summer
the music practice from the great hall
    the listeners in a stone tower pressed against
the silence that shifts
    of voices and music and lumpy winds brimming with insects
more was crossed out in the ensuing months
    attempts abandoned in favour of gruesome inertia
the flat blue surface of the swimming-pool
    collecting a grim smear of debris
fantasy of absence being the work of after-image
    fragments of letters and conversations   unread books
being part of "the story so far"
    everywhere the given condition set against the personal
desire for something difficult to explain
    but under constant and systematic examination
pacing the tiled margin
    waiting for the swimmers to surface with a splash
and gasp a greeting through the listless air
    sufficient to check the specular disaster
of the merging ripples   a situation fraught with clashing symbols
    and the suggestion of renewed hope

                              20 December 1971

you do not believe in the wall
overgrown with pressed flowers
ornamental relatives
and rectangular memories

you are wary of the stairs
with their brief and jarring levels
that dare the effortless push
towards a smouldering point where
horizontal forces converge and
hysterical distortions deflate
the armchair and the painted screen
and the spongy panic that contracts

a gloved hand passing the pill
of sugar-coated illusions

20 December 1971

before sleep you notice
the greening sky
a brittle and glittering skim off
absorbing our comments
explorations and dubious meanings
our attention is requested at random
and surprising intervals
a pleat in the fabric of the curtain
of our conversation
where ever we are
the proportions of the storm left them
gasping at the sheer force of rain
the sea repeats itself you said
along the rim small groups sat
looking into the mist
that curved into the stones
at their feet   the squish of waves
on shingle
they departed with a shudder
rising to the blue uplands
where the ruins waited thick with history

29 JANUARY 1972

standing in open space confidently
wears the air like a stretched glove
stroking the bleached and placid sky
with carefree manipulations
the room remained immobile
a cracked cup on the shelf with the biscuit tin
as they came closer we could see that they were laughing
and we did not understand the implications
of their diminishing calm
invisible shifts of light
across the strangely active surface of fatigue

17 FEBRUARY 1972

dear reader this was to have been a letter
but the day brighter and faster than first imagined
intercepted the intention
and a jelly of decisions numbs the maybe policy
usually adopted
a searching glance reveals all we expect
and many fail to surface from the consequences
of the strange narrative
within range the rumoured sequel predicts
the greater obstacle of the critical hours
having departed officially we need only arrive
to sink that sensation to the frigid depths
and rise dripping at the margin of a lyrical rush
dull epics are breaking apart at the most breathtaking
moments as our instructions solidify and take effect
we also spent some time discussing childhood memories
and how a shift has placed our new life to one side
as though the parcel had loosened
releasing its contents to the freedom of loss
    on the way
the window overlooks the unkempt garden
and the tubes of paint are getting squeezed suggestively
wish you were here
signed the frazzled correspondent

19 MARCH 1972

Cameo

the radio excuses our dawdling
a plastic alibi protects dreaming statuary
tonight you feel you may never talk again
that sense of self-indulgent excess
the notion strikes you as real
although improper
just because it's late and the lights are turned
off and we're not out
on the streets
being deserted by intention
staring avidly at the huge and godless prickle of stars
at work with the irreconcilable adversary
we are to ourselves

3 AUGUST 1972

the former arbiter cruises slowly
out of sight
breaking through proves difficult
a cupboard against the wall big as a small room
at the telegraph office there is no reply
the weekend party having dispersed raggedly
hooked off the edge of the plateau in a grand style
resting exhausted and perspiring
and emotionally weakened
no one seems to have considered the implications
that still express an inviting view of the true facts
another hasty departure
staggers full tilt across the afternoon
the distance remains
inexplorably sloping off as the view of the horizon
that rests on the window-sill

           4 AUGUST 1972

a cleaned-out sensation passes around the room
it was like walking in the forest for an instant
the crowd pressing back into nervous leaves
the open windows hold the rancid air
a door opens below the ceiling naturally
inviting a pensive mood with accompanying insects
hurtling around the light
performing small velocity upheavals
the footpath followed a shallow incline
to the next introduction on red tiles
breaking from the restless cajoling
you extend your hand as the clouds fumble
over the village
and I carry the white jug to the tap
the rain falls with such force a fine spray rises
and mist fills in the details
but the cat undeterred pads across the roof
beside the chair the pages lie unworked
curling in the sun

28 FEBRUARY/11 AUGUST 1972

Projections (1977)

the first restless flaws of morning
wipe darkness from the window
a deliberate gesture
that rewards your attention
with unhindered eloquence

here a line that seemed to stifle
the purpose
has been deleted
and now the idea departs
slamming the day in your face

11 FEBRUARY 1974

the voice is a moment
lit from behind

its shadow falls between
two surfaces now and then

this is not a welcome
but please come in

strange fixations burst
through the door

it should be who was expected
but another delight materializes

at the corner of a smile
there is determination

now the fun has really started
but there's no-one home

when they leave you catch a wave
gliding in the corner of your eye

26/28 FEBRUARY 1974

Changes
For Michael Palmer

heaviness transformed
an alert unfolding
she steps from the shadows
her name has changed
the strangeness of her ways
is nothing more
than the strangeness
of her ways after all
personal details remain elusive
the scraps of paper
that precede this
notes bleed from the aimless pen
the sky changes
temperate wind distorts the cumulus
and tarnished blades of sunlight
and the day installs its memory
and what you remember
may well have happened

        27 DECEMBER 1972

technology idles below the window
and something forgotten returns
in the way sounds rise from ground level
through swift intrusion of diluted air
to whisper the name of their hidden tormentor
forced to compromise at last
the staircase remains bright
bearing the rise and fall with placid resignation
gathering vibrant rays
dispersing them obliquely across the angle
of two legs climbing

                                              20/22 MARCH 1974

Travelling

the wilderness turns up again
and you turn away

having embarked on a journey
you arrive at its sequel

the sun blossoms overhead
dazzling your eyes

when you admit "I am lost"
we take it to mean you feel immune

and the days absorb that remoteness

July 1974

sparked off more than once before
sweating out the fever of our discontents
looking over the shoulder of the new arrangement
such breath-taking views and indiscretions
with the buxom idea and the reflex action

a siege transfixes the situation
within the column of mangled air
that rubs coarse cloud across the faded surface
the sky presents
offering a relaxing swerve into quieter
less populated areas

all this seemed as reminder for the invisible
memories to step forward with unseasonable simplicity
and claim the straying thoughts
from where they jostle with equally unseasonable gnats

but not from any false sense of duty
or respect for historic fact
just a gathering in of what once appeared too bleak
and best laid aside and forgotten
to accompany what I already possess of myself
both known and unknown   and merely guessed

27 DECEMBER 1972

Introductions

you are here and here and you are
your name

sometimes a definition and sometimes
a mistake

you are your own worst enemy
and occasionally a conflict will persist for days

without victory or defeat
sometimes your name emerges

from between the lines and sometimes
the lines themselves are its only disguise

your own company is often sufficient
a companion to entertain the four walls

their poise is controlled and reassuring
addressing you with familiarity

if friends arrive you are pleased
to see them

and it seems the walls stand back
releasing your name

August 1974

Holidays

the surroundings are pushed aside
by sleepy scribbles
a rolled window blind
releases the gloomy room
certainly we are as unreal to you
as we are to ourselves
as the day is
from a different angle
newly hauled across the view
whichever way we look
gaining a true account of the morning
into which sparse rain floats on the wind
later we walk to the harbour
idle in the shops along the quay
the hours recede
the afternoon decides in our favour
a puzzle of a day of too many clues

27 December 1972

Interior : Morning
for Patrick Caulfield

you cannot tell the time by the grey light
in the window
the frame outlines a response
tempting permutations of coincidence
it would seem that some one has forgotten
to switch off the light
the underside of the yellow lampshade
a white ellipse of proof

in order to belong to what exists
both elements
light, therefore lampshade, and window
thus time, extend the dimension
that is our sense of dawn anticipated
and uneasy not working, but content
you observe the static lucidity of crystal sky
cool air pressed flat against the eye

a fixed point will also express variables
and you pass into that portion of yourself
which entertains the idea of duality
although the window is distinct and isolate
an independent level of values
the present night and your unending mornings
coexist with a hint of studied calm
as the sun breaks through to summarise

18 JUNE 1973 / 26 JANUARY 1975

Ronny's Friend

voices in the hall
are from the head-on determination
to establish
such communications as are fitting
come in said Ronny
before yesterday is out we'll settle
our planning for tomorrow
his mother seemed transparently furtive
no matter how hard his friends tried
he couldn't invent her really being there
like so many other things
that rose before him as the days broke loose
and he lost touch with his friends
and moved away from the district
not knowing how time works
with a drift of opposing systems
Ronny's friend having been conjured
by statistics and his invisible parent
who in moments of boredom
forgot the exact location
of the bureau where the extended family
lived peacefully between table mats and napkins

30 JANUARY 1973

each day is necessary and sustains
itself and us
with what we do
and what we know of
its authenticity

marbled areas of vegetation
address a view through trees
dispersed by blunt remarks
and early mist

recent foliage manoeuvres
audibly practising
the logic of photosynthesis
gathered from march contours
and the alternating light

the fragile status of gleaming air
recites its chill remarks
despite a sky arched pleasurably
above a tossed-sheets landscape

MARCH 1975

Today Backwards (1977)

Foxtrot Marathon

the redeeming factor flushes away
monstrous thoughts before they have accumulated
with sufficient force to cause damage
however   getting in closer is one way only
of seeing the situation accurately
the deeds come later   struggling
and the gesture is one you recognise
from elsewhere
memory troubling you   though not enough
to spoil the vegetable soup
or deter the bank of grey-blue clouds humming over
the eastern horizon
as if motivated by silent engines or invisible sails
sparrows hopping between the long weeds
pay no regard   not even anticipating the snow
that I expect with little basis for my supposition
except that certain details of recent events
linger as small but powerful mementoes
pushing against the sun (the clouds)
and my nerves (the memories)
the re-enactment of a colossal drama (the recent event)
holy smoke! he exclaimed as the whole scene
went up in flames
benign smiles collapse from the frivolous tableau
of malicious glances that rapidly fade
to the obscure pattern of a blur

sitting here how do they know where
you are   or care   or why
how easy it all seemed   how trackless
if it was hope   it was a vague commodity
and lethal
we know this   and continue
around the periphery of the floor
a draft creeps disarmingly
you step from the door and continue
where the previous line left off
never so convinced as now
placed alongside the tattered remnants
I forget which afternoon
the arrangement   that was another year
who did you think you were anyway
certainly not convincing
or else alarmed and totally beside yourself
with dreams of empty fields
and the breath of travellers arriving
meanwhile your thoughts take off
for the spent passions of the west
this is a matter of further investigation
at which it ceases to exist in your mind   that is
the wholesome aspect becomes that one you choose
to ignore

a sense of strain between times is outlandish
if accurate   within the situation it finds itself
and you   the impression that you are grateful
however the stop-lights do change
and announce a satisfaction at the lack of takers
a false development from rumours of their absence
then it's time to make a move   but when

don't check dates locations intentions commonplaces
or secretly   the old fears are suddenly old fears
you are "in" my thoughts of you   nothing exists
that is not also manifest in terms of what we are
to ourselves and others come what may
which does without checking

amazed and months later   which was then the thought
extended perhaps its way made clear   more precise
an index   inspect the cloudy parts over the hill
you see how intoxicating the question has become
wearied by the wind and the blue road
furtively meandering in a small picture

which of these do you regard as vital
suspended climax   name and address supplied
immediate response as in "negative reflex" or
a clear statement of intent   remember   any one is appropriate

fortunately there is a method, you suppose
to this erratic way of living
a vital piece of information seems to have gone
astray, but how can you know, is this
a clearly defined situation, surely not

and do perimeters bear down
can this room, its table
support the daily effort, however neat
the proposal may seem, aligned with disorder
more of the mind than the alternative

you see, the story lies
in an awkward pose of relaxation
and what else but questions are there
to the basis of a sensation not yet defined
that is the proposition forcing through

that it might be known, might answer for
the dubious intention of the coming years
haunting the white curtain that arbitrates
but no, autumn has a foot in the door
by such devices are the profiles identified

this could almost be a different place
streets that accept more than you offer
and less than you care to give
you don't feel "this is it" regardless
of the corners you turn as you approach

and how much do you owe the music
there is of course the problem of afterwards
illuminated doorways and passing cars
the visitors had only entered by chance
not too strenuous an exercise to perform

the short cut seemed promising
if only something of the route was known
planning sunlight is not a matter
for rigid principles or avoided hazards
the scope of the future increases effortlessly

    the sky suggests the sundry forces
            of a day demanding green
    brown dregs disturb your first cup of coffee
            a smell of toasting slips
    beneath the door
            in place of a letter or draft
    prompting these lines
            disrupting the sequence days later
    day's light against the window
            presenting the view beyond
    that draws you from the chair
            as though the will to explore now suggests
    an alternative previously obscure
            in which you will act
    as formal observer
            the footsteps passing below
    in darkness instead of sleep
            in place of being
    somewhere or someone else entirely

how restless they are
mending their moments
who has experienced such a construction
without prior notification

close to affection
but getting further from the location preferred

whilst stairs make mountaineers
and curtains drawn back travellers
the image is its surroundings
plus various accoutrements

put out the last cigarette
put out the light

the hush that pervades
strung out through accomplished woodland
glistening after the shower
because the morning is suitable
and a moist film damps the crisp edge
of an experienced rumour

in this frame you are alluring
and in this one playful but composed

here you are not quite sure which way
now you have moved entirely

a truth hinted
in air that stuns
where the space of you is a shape
you fill and modify
palpable substance kindled from
the hotchpotch rejected by elaborations
and brazen revelry

we can suppose then
that the image relieves itself
assuming its own form incessantly
never tiring
declaring constant truth in being

the swarthy ripples of her finger-tips
combing an indigo gentleness
from the deserted arena
to make the morning departure
against which is the loosened grip
that permits the divulgence
yet retains an option one way or another
would you have guessed such scenes
is your view this same concourse
with its devotion to order
tipped askew in a spasm of avoidance
or do you see defined
some further implication
as if say you are surrounded by chairs
but lack the subtle methods of repose

does the idea of language leave an impression
a mark for identification   is one question
somehow a right decision is slowly forming
all nature pressed back with expectation
further or later but certain and beyond doubt
that worked into meaning welcomes your eyes
to suspended announcements and definitions
fervently displayed across the horizon
of notable guess-work in a scene lacking
the entire neighbourhood
that manages to avoid the calamity
but you are there first   or think you are
and the light seems that much clearer
pierces the words in such a way that only bright spots
show through the infinite shades of meaning
which brings you to an abrupt halt   a pause
during which you venture to touch that word "infinite"
its texture depresses the flesh of your finger
and you take a line with the sole purpose of avoiding
the resultant space   consumed with relief
that bridges the distance
between that word and its textures

a tight lipped aurora
disperses the last threadbare remnants

of logic imposed by sequence
your instinct folded in a concertina crush

not advancing as it should for you
today spreads maplessness ahead of hesitation

by which you mean something transient
might step between the riffling pages

a vestige of their unease
in an otherwise tranquil bulletin

simple mobility as a baffle
that sense of being in control again

to recall listless and lost
the recent past

then it seemed that all our efforts led back
towards home
that the excursion now returned us to our real lives
and their changes, some less acceptable than others
but far enough removed to be admitted
through which absence has determined
a method of approaching the most common things
with courtesy, with some respect, with considerable awe

the subtle overtones proffered by the season
the apple trees stripped of their foliage
perished fruit suspended and intact
despite rain and wind harassments, puzzles harvest logic
the hand withheld
first by absence now by lack of motive
and the greater more pressing demands
of familiar objects we readdress and know

the view from the window
dilates the easy stages of first light
into full-blown compelling and handsome hours
and foraging birds invent a sky
in the gardens jumble of untidy shrub screens
and the wind moulds a ragged procession of clouds
reversing the dun layers of a rain drenched morning
and I watch, sitting behind glass, absently jotting

this evening I am entertained by a blackbird
the sky is mauve, violet, and the colourless blue
of darkness, this of course will be the dominant
colour, from which the light of stars
will bounce and flicker down at us
in compressed intervals that flicker knowingly
long after the song has ceased
and the dubious nostalgia has been absorbed
by the sensitive approach of twilight
and the notes are like instructions
or better still
they are a list, whilst we are listless
and good intentions, like the intention of working
from early morning into the night
have a habit of getting in the way of things
although quite what the "things" are
is not easy to define, and maybe just another excuse
you can see the difficulty
here an intriguing diagonal view catches my eye
intermittent shafts of airy light collapse, fluctuate
reform, and shimmer, as the afternoon wilts
nothing you do can alter its mechanics, or the desire
to apply these incidents
but will it be now, today
or will it be tomorrow

Battledore & Shuttlecock

the reaper sighs for springly notions
but Raphael grins a regional fruit lip grin
marked nearer fumes choke the monocyclists
"tricks refused" badge clearly displayed
quests net the lozenge permit
token news announcement credits dizzy lurch
string suits tie noble legions to their stance
the loser rises looped in dread
ah cellular mound to dome retreat
your ruby gloat circles felt blocks for walling
loose flute recites the capacity
of the mittened musician asking his permission
conductor waves the melody aside between himself
and goodbye courtyard grandeur
moatless meter strands invoke green areas
that not only tender ripples flaw sweetly
but snarl in run down creepers and reach
prolonged residual sediment mustering afloat
compact tone lest all else fail terribly
by such cabinets the lugger tacks
impelled transactions fuss and expostulate
they know hurly-burly cosmetic dotage
the gaffers dawdle primly outlandish
feeble replicas supplant innermost regions rejoicing
the rights consent by slender alarm
to relinquish annotation principles that this is
ardent thistledown croons routine palaver
audible to the junketing affections of a rake

lost oddments provoke moments of doubt
the alternatives you propose inexplicably passed over
doubts crouched behind moments you suddenly recognise
in order to propose the inexplicable without doubt

as the lost oddments pass the alternatives by
that is, with assurance, with affectionate familiarity
the wind catches the fruits of its circumstance
pushes the baggy clouds together, aloft, and underway

the circumstances are these, checked with a backwards glance
there is no wind and the sky sags petulantly
denying neglect the fruits ripen as an alternative
you've been lost before, were you found, reclaimed

found as lost you remained without place, are now searched for
colossal gusts fan out through the buttoned up darkness
thorough as a search party, loose and undulant
folded back crisply they return upon us, themselves, renewed

they are perpetual, escaping nothing
memorise certain details, they may prove of use later
regard each gesture, no matter how slight, as ambiguous
do you detect the fragile fabric of meaning

how easy now to feel perplexed, lost in the coils
of this your own plot against yourself, totally immersed
pliant to its unwinding, but you've been there before and know
the principle of inclusion is exclusive, is what next

there is enough for us all
and the days
maybe a little wearier a little less buoyant
settle to their business
as before, and yet a touch revives you
fresh, cool
the perfect example of itself
as though in lasting long enough it qualifies
for a place in your confidence, which it does
but later
and an hour has passed already
because you check
the spongy air arranged in layers
illuminating a scrupulous display of truths
that mask the names we use

Today Backwards
for John James

Friday takes a step in the right direction
towards Saturday
but first its cool evening of pleasurable dusk
house-martins swooping and turning for their perpetual dinner
and the stimulating cessation after the first
drowsy heat of summer

an hour reading lying in the sun
then I harden my heart loosen my bowels
and set to work

it is 2.00pm and gloriously fluttering green on blue
first from the window
and then across the paper
placing foliage that it might breathe
above the still and sparkling water
bearing its open surface like the glazed look
of one transfixed
that reaches you in the air above
and arranges the view reversed at your feet

an empty place is possessed by figures
only their conversations remain illusive
and we quickly occupy the lack with our imaginings

nowhere else was quite the same as today
floating between us on the gluey breeze

Fading into Brilliance (1978)

Fading Into Brilliance

Eventually it was difficult to decide where to commence, what to say, which, of the many, would be the correct invective as retaliation, how the very attempt could be justified according to the precepts established in the fabric of yesterday, rejected today. We run into dust storms that hurl gritty words at the walls of our understanding. The journeys enhance our physical bearing. We divide ourselves into the strangeness of arriving for the first time. Greetings cast a doubtful shadow over the faces of the assembled friends, who are meeting for the first time. Nigel speaks of his adventures in the glittering nights; Kevin tells of living on the coast, sucked at by trade winds, and the scrawny arm, always reaching out to him from the foundation cream of his lady's youth. What I am saying is far from the room where I believe you work. Nevertheless, pronouncements continue to inform the fictional scholars.

The arrivals took place, notes were consulted, corrections made to paradoxical texts, the truth was apparent, and that helped. The circus of knowing smiles touring the social sawdust, Also, age became at one and the same time, "of paramount importance" and, "of little significance". This was good. A reasonable balance controlled hysterical outbursts.

The crystallisation into language, and thereafter, out beyond its structures, has become part of our way of living. Notes written previously no longer apply. The difficult exercises are one more aspect of necessary communication. We delight in a fusing of disciplines, and encourage the mobility of targets. Our responsibility is clearly defined, and documented in such a way that we are better composing a euphemistic refusal, on our own terms. The headache exerts a pressure behind their eyes, the weakness bears down on them, in order that they may become strong, and provide access to those areas normally dismissed as hypothetical. We are finding our way through and no longer rely on the state of self-induced chemical dreams.

You expect total harmony and receive discord, returning at last to the practice of solitary authorship. Hidden behind a buoyant curriculum, you visit libraries and bookshops to sleep in quiet corners of forgotten sub-sections of remote departments. The radio fizzles to a silence that is international static.

The preparatory moves arrived from an altered way of living.

He accepted the brief encounter as a sign that tremendous infiltrations would benefit his future extravagances. The season closed like a clammy door against our faces. Furtherance becomes a byword in the political exchange that fills the meeting hall with breathless subjugation. We leave hastily, never to return. The books express our opinions, becoming a way of living within the structure we have established as necessary, and from where we negotiate the terms of our acceptance.

Certainly a foreboding existed. The credibility of our work was questioned only by persons from other departments. Although each was existing within a parlicular art form of considerable personal consequence. I admit to the devious problems presented in acts of sustained energy. The bondage of words, gathering as viable language, frequently closes in, with a forced conclusion only extremes of concentration betray, and the mind runs on, towards a dubious future. We are allowed our emptiness and moments of strikingly magnetic vacancy. At times a divine non-communication relates all we wish to offer to the collective question. The silence develops into a common need and our greetings crackle finely in the charged air. I am waiting for the sudden reversal of images. Looking for a new life cancels nothing. Only the effortless practice of your craft marks you out, and that apparent ease must not deny the complexity of continued striving.

You are walking from the newsagents with a line between your eyes, repeating the words, committing to memory, hurrying back to write them onto a filing card.

Wherever the clues take us, we will travel and be content, it is partly a matter of thought, and partly an activity of the hands. A body gains access to the gloomy bedroom of our adventure. We cannot identify the sex, it is of little consequence. Some believe

Kevin has returned, others, that those were the thighs of vivacious Isabel. No one is to know, finally. We are leaving. The moon leans over the enchanted garden.

The spell of journeying is exceptional. A memento stands on the shelf. The future faces us squarely, inviting a collection of new decisions.

By now the purpose was quite clear, and utilising each of its components we settled down to the work required of us, encouraging ourselves with greetings and farewells, writing letters to the future with increased regularity. The mountaineers descended to read the works in manuscript. Divers gurgled up from the bay. I now find sleep disturbs the engrossing activity and winter sends its nights in dark packages. The sun glances through the sky with a meagre wave, a shallow arc. Our thoughts lock on sound effects. The clarity expresses itself in detailed reports. Accomplishment springs into place, and we are obliged to grasp and hang on. The knowledge is available and we know this, as, daily, we move towards it, fading into brilliance.

The Adventure

Meanwhile the delighful conclusions diminish. An attempt at recovery was successfully thwarted in the early stages, leaving only the vagueness of historical speculation. Wasted effort falls aside limply. The garden is ignored and grows back quickly to wildness and fond entanglement. The mass of the air delights us as it moves, playfully, against our bodies. A thrill travels with us in the form of our profiles. We know we will be eternally grateful. All the spare parts have arrived and only await the fitting.

They introduce themselves as old friends from a former time, and tell us the dates and how the weather was. The house seemed dark, we held back the curtains and nothing happened. Sometimes we don't know where we are, but that's not a bad thing really, if we consider the vast confusion available to us, in which to perform our getting lost. So much can be mislaid in this way. Certainly the chances of loss are as numerous as those of finding the most appropriate route; although little is known of the differing characteristics, and many get through without knowing.

The personnel are lined up, waiting to move in, to make this a telling narrative. They are preparing for an introduction. Our perverse determination is to exclude their influence on what is becoming important to our intentions. Such persistence is commendable but misplaced. We are not looking for a faithful entourage. We have other plans and inspect our destiny with chilling calm. You would be wise to ignore the plea, they wish only to perpetrate a ragged continuance of some fiction they insist is their life. Collective adventures, idols of foldaway book stands. We are not so foolish as to dismiss totally a reality we doubt through inexperience. You are touched by this forbearance, and the comet curves majestically across the clear night sky. A new religion snarls into action in the vaults of perverse financiers.

Ralph's glowing beauty lights Nigel's cigarette and sparkles in the facets of the cut-glass goblets on the ivory inlaid ebony table. Their assignment complete they relax in Dale's apartment, awaiting the official clearance and tickets for Bermuda. Roger and Norman drive to the coast in Isabel's car. The house is vacant for the winter months. Cynthia is due to arrive in three days. Her husband divulges useless secrets to an alien power. The chief of police, ignoring Robert's monologue, changes to the mad professor. A computer deciphers the plans. No-one is leading a normal life. A sign of the times dismisses their extravagances.

Looking up from our books, metaphorically, we become aware of the turn things have taken, without our knowledge. The adventures that have commenced unassisted. Our delay has been crucial, we sit on deck with our martinis as the cargo boat sails determinedly into the oyster sunset. Ah well . . .

We scrutinise the situation and discover there is a long way yet to go. We have no notion of where we will stand in relation to the way of living that has extended beyond our lives to become a part of the very fabric of our fragile existence from day to day. The desire is that we will get through intact with the bulk of our work to state the realism we had attempted to confirm. Should we so wish certain of our letters will be mounted and set under glass, alongside rare butterflies and gross biological extremes. Having untied the knot of our days we are left with the daunting task of gathering and ordering them as we would wish to see them best represent our attitudes.

Systems tell us that which we don't always wish to know or be part of. Most often we are not, being extraneous matter to such calculated processes. Fish rise glibly beneath the bulbous fluorescent floats, and rods dip towards the ripples. A bather springs into the icy water with a loud and painful smack! Dirk visits Nigel. Ralph's jealousy extinguishes the eternal cigarette.

In our work we demand an undivided attention. The comedians make the profit. Tomorrow, whatever is settled will be taken as the next step. Conversations of a dubious nature to holding hands.

The differences wander freely between our points of reference until without our knowledge the one becomes the other and we no longer recognise the truth. Facts are in dispute. We still have that on our side, although things familiar are ignored totally, and strangers share our food like old friends. All the previous records are stored neatly in boxes and mean nothing in the light of our recent discoveries. Asked for definitions we are rendered speechless, fumble for a phrase, a single and communicative statement. The air shakes. I introduce myself from the shadows and sit quietly at a nearby table, careful not to make any noise that might disturb them before my chosen moment will obliterate their sensationalism.

A card arrives. You are greeting us from a distance that refuses our traffic in mute gestures. More is to be hoped for in the eventuality of our game being successful. Cynthia destroys the rule book leaving the others in a state of nervous collapse. They were relying on the event as a means of providing fashionable and compelling distinctions, this was to have been the climax. Frustration and disappointment giggle in the corner. Their efforts at commandeering the plot have failed. Suddenly it is the memory of what may have been a struggle impresses on us the very temporariness of the escapade, bound up as it has been, with our desire to establish some truth, no matter how devious and awkward, to admit its presence in the core of the not entirely sequential narrative. But enough was enough, left as we then were to tidy the storm damage. Such havoc was an uncommon site for the ensuing nostalgia. The sigh entered our lives forcefully and without prior warning. Even now we laugh at the remembered spectacle.

Delighted by the future occasions we arrive thankfully. Having made the effort we find the labour rewarded with vast murmurings. Those we knew before remain in the vaguer context, sitting along the edge of an ancient and faded recollection. The events swoop backwards along the dark tubes of yesterdays and the dry touch of an ultimate conclusion flakes off into isolation. We look back with fondness on the reliable changes. So much of what is to happen charges our idea of the future with accurate predictions.

The Spring-Loaded Cash Drawer

The delicate gesture disintegrates in the vibrant air. He is already too far away and mere shouts melt inadequately from the occasion. You dust the shelves of sleep lightly, fully resigned to a treatment of expressionless medicines. His timetable admits no variables. The paradoxical "incident" will be imposed by chance. A strange fancy settles on the crêpe hillside. The pattern of behaviour has no precedent, gathering vast forces of decaying laughter behind a screen. A mark of some significance appears on the page hastily pasted to a bill-board in an obscure location. Getting through the gate of stars and paper shapes is one way of expressing your bewilderment. The proprietor deals with the customer in an unusually benevolent manner, chatting and laughing over the spring-loaded cash drawer. Evidence points to a confusion of acceptable proportions. Denials take the place of reason. Birds inject the calm morning with the oddity of their ways. To underline their dramatic heritage they swoop into the sky with its trimming of gruesome, childlike clouds. His return was forecast daily until the officials censored further announcements, "in the light of information received. Which we are not at liberty to disclose, at the present time." Rumour identified him as the informer, exaggerating his continued absence. At any moment the telephone was expected to ring. An air of expectancy was established that had been unequalled since the postmen's strike. Right now we are confident of a great degree of the accuracy that is characteristic of the proof to corroborate our assumptions. He is certainly within range. The evidence points to his having infiltrated, and established a base at, the heart of the organisation's area of activity. A frantic and untidy search disturbs the campaign. Postures collapse in folds and clouds of powder. He has invented a life-style of dubious value and rides supremely in the limousine of his imagination. Returning in the fringe hours to a cold room, the gas-fire and the extravagant pen poised over the invitation card. The party had suffered from rash conclusions. They all, without exception, departed flamboyantly, concerned with the dramatic effect of their individual activities. The outrage was no more than a trigger. Solemn air currents turn the key in a cloudy door. Despite the new arrivals they continue to play the role of respected celebrities. Elusive and dramatically phlegmatic he retires to his room above the bakery, in heavy disguise. The soft surging wells from the desk. He advances lightly over the seaweed. The storms rest noisily in the locked cupboard. Already the estimates have doubled with a gesture of frothy confusion. The sense of ease lies across a chair with the various components of the disguise. Wilful deeds collect on the forceful contents page, each with its serial number and sense of place. Brought forward into the light, suddenly and startlingly revealed, the episode seems less drastic, not so fraught with obscure foreboding. Further developments press for the serialisation rights, assuming various stances and encouraging cameo poses. Negotiations are held in abeyance.

Getting Through The Door

Enamel signs glint in the light of our discoveries. The loss is elsewhere. For the declaiming critics their miserable failure is their own concern, fumbling at the distinct edge of a sparkling accomplishment. Severity inspects previous tolerance and advocates the hard line. Much is cancelled as the margins darken with graffiti and new functions are discovered. Authenticity remains firm against the squall of suspect derivations. We tried biting the smile from the back of our heads. Shaking a hand wildly towards the standard hello. Whatever the sensation was, the room contained its essence. Not necessarily explicit in terms of enclosure, but of value nonetheless. Being remote turned up again. An evaluation gave out gracefully before the questionable solution extablished a constancy.

Fixing the lamp made some of the room quite real. Throwing light into exhausted faces. The spiral of black flex from the ceiling to the white shade. Plainly the intangible atmosphere claimed them as its source, each giving off a nervous aura of expectation.

Whilst talking animatedly from a new set of experiences the undercurrent swirls with a system of mysterious changes. How gaily the discussion hurls forwards. Planning how they might react to each other reacting to us; or we, in reciprocation, would cause them to examine our motives, our assessments going on past the occasion towards later discussions.

The conversation held back from itself, ill at ease in the testing of socio-political notions we had not expected from this direction, and hinged at a point that has not been familiar to us. It seemed that what remained outside the context of where the words were aimed, became the subject of the exchange. It was towards some previous occasion that the curious glances would stray, deflecting off a sudden shield of dialogue.

Slowing down pushes against the tongue's effort. The troublesome commitments of a previous generation activate the door. What we lay aside will represent nothing less than a twisted wreckage of insoluble situations. The departure leaves them with the disadvantage of not knowing what we now puzzle over, surrounded by the interconnections of a surprise visit.

Static Journey

The way the days fray at the edges and meet disturbingly gives a truer sense of the passage of time than we have previously been aware of, although it has existed quite blatantly as the dates indicate and has undergone its progression of changes unmolested by our new and curious demands. The abundance of ideas has quite spontaneously developed into a real need for certain answers to the questions that have recently arisen as the result of misleading and eventless contemplation. If we had thought to outgrow these intense feelings, or let them accumulate and sit accusingly in a corner, we had reckoned without consideration or acceptance of those desires that remain dormant for only a limited period of time, to be triggered into action by some word of unlikely image or searching glance. The invented selves step through the door and our problem is to determine their identity and function. Having placed the various results beside the remnants of feeling, we are able to look back calmly over what has passed knowing the inherent strength of our weaknesses. The garden steps away gracefully, and you look from the window at your staring face. To come from sense of enclosure to sense of breaking apart we thrust a flapping hand into the fragments. You are constantly traversing all manner of events and experiences, and step into such occasions with newly acquired skill. The basic act of continuance has become the ultimate intention, and the aim consolidates to form a nucleus of energy. From the terrifying ooze of a forced cessation, the overt parallelism and drowsy discomfort, the ennui melts off, suggesting a clarity we are soon to witness.

An Adventurous Episode Rejected By Boys Own Paper

Somehow we are attending to the demands of a fertile imagination. Back at headquarters you decide on the course of action that will conclude the exercise. He rests in the tall wicker chair placed beneath the boughs of an apple tree, disturbed by wasps and huge sneezes. The narrative continues with a glance in his direction and the shouts of the cast echo in the beams and trusses of the warehouse. You approach from shadows, muttering instructions. Familiar faces apply for the names listed on the notice board. The signature of the official is indecipherable. One way to proceed would be to extend the activities of those who belong here. A graph to verify what is not apparent, or seems confused with eventfulness, serves only to baffle those seeking a choice of entertainment. Progress translates as a moving away from what was established in earlier reports. Your own idea seems less precise, disappears with eagerness. The assistance of those others threatens to absorb what remains of the thread of your intention. They claim to be what remains. You send the plans and instructions by special messenger and telephone to establish welcome. An unsigned letter falls into the wrong hands. They have wired the darkness to a giant receiver. Their sinister presence disturbs the company of heroes who wait for the final order. You and he look much alike and introduce yourselves with the aid of a full-length mirror, where others are waiting repetitively to invade the room. Our foibles are enough to occupy the thoughts of those who require clues. The process undergoes a degree of change, each system being entirely original yet bearing the unmistakeable mark of familiarity. A motor starts and gently recedes into the clouded distance, rubbing your ears with its vibrations. It is the only indication of activity, or the existence of some other person, outside the room where you write this report in fear and desperation. You pause, misguided, but not entirely led astray. We understand the pressures you have been subjected to and compose a series of letters of condolence and encouragement that are quite irrelevant.

Certain facts come to light, due to the vigilance and astute deductions of our agents, that poise before us menacingly, before departing with a gassy fizz. The column of weary travellers returns to its reward of societies and encyclopedic anecdotes. You expect an invitation that fails to arrive, and receive further orders in a code of strip cartoons.

Another factor sets oul to surround what seems merely the exercise of establishing the mode of existing we believe will place us within the decisive and linear strategy we recognise as our life. The tendencies are flexible and reshape the wake of your sudden unfurling. An irritation stitches discomfort behind your eyes. Incomplete, we stand with friends, alone, waiting, huge and mumbling in the deluge, the claustrophobia of comic dreams.

The report is submitted for their attention, and later set aside with resignation. The outrage and protests direct a vicious glance. Oh music! it seeps through the air, neutralising the malicious stridencies. Whatever we are is also today a thing of the past. They stumble along close to the wall, set out into the total gloom, your perverse hands placed in erotic spaces, without reference to possible guidance. You are here and growing closer, as you discover less and less of what there is to know, and gain that intelligence reserved for strangers who live a life of tight disorder. You look through your years with a sense of loss and satisfaction, not merely the standard sigh of resignation. The discussions about the plateau expedition are ruling your days.

Several scenes occurred within the span of what we have now encompassed with our theory of definition. A setting sun illuminates the lady cyclist, and the first signs of change in the dense foliage. Horizontal rays. Are these the endorsement required to verify the linear hypothesis? Is is it to be the one whose tender look lingers at the edge of the spectacles, dependent, of course, on the wearer? The mysterious transaction that will provide a key to the entire puzzle is arranged furtively, behind locked gates, in a deserted vegetable garden at the perimeter of the town, an unfamiliar area where many of the

Edwardian villas are falling asleep, bored with the task of housekeeping. The contact faces you across a tea-table set with china cups, saucers and plates of the Ming dynasty. Having dispensed with introductions the verbal exchange commences. It is your friendship with angels and pilots that has made all this possible, he says, a more than adequate reference. And I now feel able to transfer my secret without fear of reprisal. I only wish to assist you with the task at hand. We must have complete confidence in each other, total trust. You see the success of this mission relies on a recall of the most inconsequential details. Such minutiae as the tap of a foot, creak of a chair in the framework of the plan, gasp of a maid bending at the keyhole of the study door, goosed by the Major, again and again, unable to straighten from that intense crouch, distant hoot of the 7.45, dull scrape of tea-cups and a sugar bowl in the gruesome cafeteria, and the apparent innocence of the swarthy stranger who will later be identified. The wind placed a chill embrace. Was it nausea signalled the presence of some acidic malfunction in the shrubbery, reminiscent of the confusion with the list of names? Now it all seems a posed device. You had never really accepted the role of all-rounder and everybody's standby in the wings. A fine time to take off, he muttered, a sardonic grin twisting his lips like a can-opener. By now it was quite dark and only the glowing tip of his cigarette served to prove his existence. And what form of a reality is that?

It had indeed been a time of considerable confusion. Shuffling from one foot to the other, as if ideas were stones, or some such metaphor. The nervous aspects of the days a symptom of their public face, made certain adjustments to our way of regarding the problem of who would become first person singular, should a final outcome prove essential to the satisfactory completion of the narrative. This arises as the central, or pivotal, point we entertain as the honoured guest. The need to identify and take stock, which lately has assumed the form of a resigned knowledge that the endeavour is an endless performance of striving. Then the question of the placing of that external force, circumstance, set a turbulence in motion, at which point you close the report.

Nothing Is Abstract

The difference, being quite distinct, accepted the conclusion we now thought fitting for such marked originality of intention. Our only desire submerged beneath the greater expanse so artfully exposed, and sharp with a definition extracted from the fertile air and our age. Understanding too comes with slight sideways motion, taking its position of intent as yet another facet of the overall knowledge.

The footpath is spongy and ill-defined beneath layers of moss, deadening the sound of footsteps hurrying from the ruins that push through encroaching foliage, the whole having an aspect of iridescent green. A summer had settled the matter, stimulating our desire for long walks and breakfasts at dawn. A year had passed over the pages with the speed and ability of a magician's hand. What was forgotten breaks sweetly into the forefront of things mostly lacking in delight at being here, which is still that place we have always turned to for its lack of identity, offered as an enticement to our sense of discovery.

Only the most arresting and momentous occasions are capable of lurching to their feet amidst the mass of reclining memories. However, the sun established its dominance and emphasised those colours of the season that succeed in filling you with an annual dose of awe, nostalgia for a now uncertain past that has become as unpredictable as what will inevitably follow the present course of events, and impatience for the brutal rigours of winter, this latter for its promise of spring.

True, much was influenced by the ache above your eyes, settled there without appointment, irritating and stubbornly persistent, but the creamy clouds, inflated from the horizon and hidden valves, muffled the silver-blue glare of the sky, seeming to enclose and absorb the pain.

Now we see the extent of our vision up ahead. The understanding allowed to those who remain is entirely created from conjecture. How are we then to respond without a full account of all that has become encompassed. At night the windows turn in upon our activities, dark mirrors that emphasise the surrounding spaces. With this in mind you return to the hollow world where structures represent nature and man, and the wisdom that they create. Nothing is abstract. The context in which we work is total in its affiliations with freedom. But the very divergence that set this analysis in motion is even now leading us away.

The Strategy

More and more the meaning of what is now taking place forms as a tangible unit, achieving substance and purpose, proposing further episodes, recording what occurs with brilliant and accurate detail. The unification of fiction and daily events, the response of one to the other, a homage to all who tread their span with feet placed firmly in each realm, who step at will through either state, or both.

It ought to come true. The position seems obscured by a knowledge of all that has become necessary in order to encourage the experiments in their endeavours. An arm pressed back against the chair, and jumpy with cramp, deters the pen. Closely followed by lack of purpose, or an inability to decide where attention shall rest for the few remaining minutes. Interchange. The name seems familiar and does eventually tell you all you want to know. This is forgotten. The mind is a lost property centre, filled with confusion and variety, an uneasy repose, a sensational lack of strategy. The keeper wakens to your knock and consults your request with an inquisitive glance at the ledger in order to determine its worth, and such action as may be deemed pertinent.

However, the chance find leads to further discoveries and illuminations. Consider my reaction when the parcels arrive intact and secure, bound with that hairy string I never save, but is invariably seen around such large packages. Some popularity must influence its continued use. When the storm breaks the air divides, saturated with rain. The torn wrapping flattens on the path, the fibres falling apart. When you gather its pieces and place them in the bin a strange indifference stakes a claim. The storm should lack for nothing, should advise you of the possible change, of a new arrival.

Now great determination is called for, and there is time for other reasoning, Have we simply laid waste our idea of the ultimate statement, knowing our foundation on such precepts comes not from a willing desire to participate, but from the further stance of inheritance? That is, set back quite distinctly as an altar-like structure, where we find a vacuum in place of a god. And knowing this rely on our island sense of being vulnerable, which takes on the black look of great continents and applies the bleach of parody to remove the uncomprehending stain. Or more simply, and effectively, convert the element of bigotry into work.

Recycling the politics of your own smile you look up from your studies and are struck by the emptiness of the room described. Is being here an alibi? This is what you are returning to when time seems to stand, poised and perfectly balanced, between that which is yet to materialize, and the recent past, as you dream the cross-reference of a remote and distorted existence.

Risks

The only remaining thought of how the adventure might end was swiftly removed by orchestrations and worn verbal gestures from an opera none of the small group could understand, lost as they always seemed to be in an auditorium at the other, the north side, of the town. Lost as they were, in garters and heels, that other geography.

When leaving, say as little as possible, depart softly, and without looking in any direction than those allowed by the eye. The field of vision.

You wander until a new gesture attracts the density of your desire towards the outward. Having closed that door move simply, and with ease, to the next. Too damn right you win! Follow those dreams, theories and sensitive perceptions that have come to mean so much in your life. A reasonable enough approach to the matter of doubt.

You are conscious of an attractive and compelling desire to make contact. The shower has ceased, leaving a huge space of aquamarine blue, fringed with sparkling cloud. Everywhere is sharply defined and glistening with a film of moisture. You arrange a meeting for the following afternoon on the steps to the entrance of the deserted auditorium. You glance at the window where you know she will be practising, working on the music that, even now, will ensnare you. It must have been around this time that you first felt an overpowering dislike for the opera.

Once the decision is formulated you prepare to establish the means by which you will gain favour in order to carry out the plan to its full extent. But it is this very purpose, so fresh and exact, deters your impulse for action. What is needed is . . . The truth of your action lies in the . . . A safe distance must be maintained between . . . Whoever appears first shall have the full benefit of . . . The locality has since become far too public and will require . . . Motives are an essay in the . . . Hot flushes damage the cool scenes and . . . For this reason we are not at liberty to divulge the source of our information, but can say . . . Having approached the problem thus far you reach for an enlightened ... Displaced yet eradiating confidence that ...

Of course your presence in the room is a new condition, one that has existed as a part of the mysterious outcome of future events. Always it had seemed overwhelmed by what occurred in the daily timetable. Now you can see it as it is, or has become, due to ignorance of its imminent fulfillment. And the day too, fanning the action with warm winds and cloudy sunlight suggests a proximity to Autumn. A faint amber flash. A prediction in browns that settled along edges how many hours ago? Is this impression false? Is second person singular someone closer to home? Are you now prepared to undergo a simple process of elimination, leading into a state of understanding, the possible, perhaps the only outcome of what has been set down? I settle, in agitation, for a brief pause ...

Second Chance

In the room above, the blank and dateless diary awaits a first entry. It will not be today. Sometimes the intention slips against a barrier you are unable to breach, shaking you with a pressure that seems to recall implications of catastrophe. For those who continue there is a way of living we no longer discuss. The plan you have developed for breaking loose exists in harmony with a chaos of mind that exerts an influence you sometimes feel may result in the current work being several pages shorter than desired. But what is that mysterious threat? A bank of cloud waltzes across the earnest blue sky. At least you are fully aware that a second chance is not what is required, and is slightly distasteful.

Breathless and weary from such strangeness, their comments regarding the existence of a "powerful influence" misrepresent all you have established in the last years. More than ever before delay sickens you; a sense of real time is apparent, it is Monday, and a year later you place the remembered event against what is now taking place. Hanging the newly framed screenprint "Interior: Morning". The light still burning against a grey restrained dawn. A constant reminder of the first minutes of each day. You are astonished. The open door sways slightly in the breeze. You are astonished, and shiver. The sun shines through the yellow blind. The page is reduced in proportion to the words. You suddenly feel determined to carry on.

Examining The Earthworks

That was long ago, or once, upon a time, or similar opening gambit. And the gift was more a coincidence than a considered, carefully and judiciously selected present. Anyway it's what became of them that really matters. Had there not been a certain air of trepidation? Aerial photographers provide far more kite images than earth configurations. In the birch copse further evidence came to light of early settlement. The footpath crossed his arm, turning sharply and rising along the outstretched fingers. At this rate the journey and the sun should complete their day's business simultaneously. Pebbles had been collected from the shore and transported inland to be used as ammunition against invaders. One theory proposes the unit so formed would establish an anthropological link between the main parts of the structure. Considered opinions contest the validity of this premise. Anyway the drastic measures are once more casting lots, and shadows, and a line, gold ingots, off. Then too, the third person strides along the skyline ahead of us, where we had thought to be alone. He is searching for similar evidence. The whereabouts of an impending confrontation with the author of a certain document, whose recent concerns had excluded any possibility of collaboration. Having reached the road they strode off in the most obvious of opposite directions.

Never Let It End

When the first part made its presence known we were not prepared, although somehow remained calm, but anxious, until it seemed this was what all previous signs must have been indicating and the positive side acted as a kind of stabilizer to the fact of our not really having been aware of anything we might seriously have assumed to be a sign. Nonetheless the matter seemed clearer if viewed in this way and we settled back with our knowledge to begin the process of interpretation. On good days the work seemed total and quite singular, glittering with a richly hued originality, but this naive and unrealistic view of things was always diluted by the bad days. No particular direction and page after page torn slowly and depressingly into strips. However! And that was no sure antidote. Briefly, our work was divided into sections and handed out at random for a personal interpretation. The most common method was that of the three-dimensional grid, where no system was fixed and the operator chose according to his own requirement, whether the move should be vertical or horizontal, forward or the reverse.

He watched from the window, observed the garden colour slowly in the dawn, the idea pushing light into the room behind him and over the table where the work lay, waiting. The journey back. They had followed the most direct route. Certainly the urgency had been largely dispelled, allowing the event's bizarre direction to filter through his awareness of it. The window filled with immense demonstrations of gleaming sunlight. Between sentences he pauses to sketch a detail of the landscape drawn on the page, intermingling with words and punctuation, a room expands in such a way that the view is enclosed by the frame of the window above the table on which he works. In the sketch the table-top is clear of obstructions. Several lines later more detail is filled in: an open note book, papers in an uneven pile, a small reading lamp with flexible arm and fluted metal cowl, a glass ashtray, a pen. All on the page on the table in the room where he works, by the window.

Various avenues to explore. We work on several levels simultaneously. He is unable to maintain a continuity, disintegrating into the facets of the day and night that swarm in his head, exposing a series of startling alternatives on the page where the ink, changing colour, implies that a modification has occurred in the quality of the light. Once before the dawn had grown into his understanding of such a situation, but no memory is certain to contain the entire assemblage of detail when later recalled or compel with quite the same intense ardour such avid response. The narrow encrusted footpath as far as the roses. A spangle of moisture along the edges of the leathery leaves. The neglected mansions are bleached slowly by the process of age, shrinking under the burden of their experiences. The silenced rooms become dense with waiting. When the doors are opened a sigh chokes hoarsely from the cranked hinges. The sudden attention to catch the slightest impression of former dealings. A panorama of images drifting sedately through the haze, intent on decorating the view from the page.

The Last Pages

What begins in mid-sentence is the half filmed gesture, the incomplete response, that will translate by means of a series of diagonal shifts, as the conclusion fidgeting for its place. A blue sky is boxed by the overwhelming activities that describe the day.

The activity zone transmits portions of the event in accordance with the rate of action. Imagine the zone as a disc into which parabolic curves intrude; the segment of the disc enclosed by the arc becomes that part of the event perceived by that parabola. The parabola's name is Edmund. A further parabola, William, an intimate friend of Edmund, not only occupies a portion of the activity zone, but also interlocks with Edmund's experience. Here then we have a mutual adventure; and this principle embraces the lives of Nigel, Cedric, Ronald, Fay, Amelia, Fenella, Henry, Doris, Fred, Samantha, Gloria, Hubert, and you.

The question of who you are is then transcribed as "progress into the bluish dark". And progress is slow. But now you can detect a certain tremulous movement forwards, particularly apparent in the comment "I believe you are real, that you too exist". The you of "you", and the other, pressured into one, discharging duplicate energy, qualify as present focal point. The rain has stopped now, we can continue. The question of who you are is closely allied to the purpose of the journey. You are travelling home, the latest excursion completed to your total satisfaction, the papers concerning this neatly stored in a manilla folder in the bag by your side. With such grist for the mill you have provided the required escape clause, and can now think of those other concerns that have remained dormant during the recent conundrum.

Amelia and Doris are passengers on another train of thought, Henry is the attendant who will deal quietly and efficiently with their requirements. Fay and Fenella fumble with Fred, whose recent discoveries, which are of a personal nature, have expanded his views and attitudes to various practices that have hitherto been excluded from his activities.

Meanwhile we are bypassed by a throng of other events. People moving from place to place, purposeful and intent. Their strategy one of daily routine that encompasses premeditation and spontaneity.

A car splutters, revs and settles to its journey. The light hurts your eyes after a day in the sun. The groceries cost more each time you shop. A certain distance from this idea is waiting to be traversed; what has this to do with the car? Free associations and systems of personal volition can be considered as one way of representing substance.

Does the will to explain desert, losing the struggle, finally, for mastery over hot divisions? In what has preceded you see only the slow, silent, ambiguous collapse of the hero. At last.

All the places you can imagine, and more besides.

"Twenty-four hours ago I was just a man with a mission" Cedric announced. She looked at his quarry grey face, perplexed, and somehow void of purpose. Her eyes glistened with moisture, "Oh Seedy" she sobbed, "I knew our love was doomed. Why did we have to meet under such circumstances? Must this be the last time?" "It can be no other way for us." An edge of bitterness sullied his words. He turned and walked from the room into the night and the finale of the story. Her tears splashed freely into his untouched martini. With movements that seemed automatic and calculated she removed a small revolver from her lamé evening purse, and placed it beside the glass. Trickles and rivulets of rain crawled down the window, distorting her reflected movements, superimposed on the view across the forlorn and deserted park.

Much of what now determines the outcome is conceived in the systematic programming of alternatives. These are sometimes present, sometimes absent. What you are writing stalls. You regard the conflict of intentions. To continue requires a retreat. In this way you are able to interrupt those elaborate moments of panic that persist and bleach the mind of its recollections. So it can be seen, that to extend the work one has to leave the room;

not to arrest the process, but to fabricate a maze through which the diverted idea may travel.

Now the slow approach, its breathing space, the quietness, begin to enclose all the separate ideas and their actions. Looking back tells little of how it was then, those first words placed in an absent-minded way on the page and that they should lead here, to this, to its own conclusion that is, the conclusion of itself. Like tying up the loose ends, sorting the sheets, assigning numbers so that they might gain the advantage of a fragile continuity; giving order or expulsion to those hazardous and self-indulgent exercises with spoof narrative. Where do they expect to coincide with the present discourse, and how maintain their campy titillations? After all, our appetites are becoming jaded with such a prolonged absorption of conflict, double-take, vacillation, eroticism and heart burn after pink gins at the club. This too must cease. The answers given reduce each question to a detail of the previous concerns, those that are no longer evident, having retreated from the area of conflict that now assumes the pose of assorted fortunes left wallowing in the furtive wake of our emerging. And we know we are our doubts; given credence and the will to retain their native enigma, allowing one to retain the other's loss.

Rising early, the washed sky brightens and releases the day with a rush. Placed then, at the edge of experience, you proceed cautiously, following the fine demarcation between all that has been forgotten, and an awareness of that fact. And the light, sleeping behind objects now defined, wrests itself from the shadows, commencing the placement of folds, rifts and tucks in the land. All these seemingly commonplace events contrive to place the wholeness of the day before you; it then becomes your responsibility to provide the necessary impetus for your action and interaction with its accomplishment, to fashion the events that will later replace the notion of "another day another dollar".

Should the day become organised around the core of your regard for it, or is itself, alone and agreeable to you, then it is its prerogative to entice your attention from the loosened and variable portions of the plot. That it can no longer persist as episodes without artificial support implies that your fears are justified. As each line advances the scheme retreats, tempting a payoff. You are able to stand away from the central theme, regardless of its demands; for now the process has become self motivating, advancing and retreating with a healthy lack of preordained ambition. With each experience its will to exert an influence is absorbed by the field of your own recently acquired perceptions and in knowing this we each proceed inevitably to the next act.

Hotel Zingo (1981)

Debate

the smeared look of the day dissolves
in powdery folds
distorting images that pulsate and ripple
on the bluish glass of the door
a reserved area for optical trickery

behind my back the room softens
like a sponge immersed in water

layers of vanilla cloud move across
the perspective defying afternoon where intervals
of diluted brightness multiply

like an idea
wandering in from the curious matinee performance
smelling of the future and an icy wind
here to deliver a promise here to collect
its dues

28 DECEMBER 1972

Unable to ignore
the preposterous intrigue,
or establish its certainty, you reach
for a name.
There is no answer.
It is out of range.
The fermentation determines
the degree of productive response.
The texture of the rain
suggests snow.
A swarm of dull reflections
locked in a window you suspect
conspires with the blurred particulars.
The day goes on and on,
obsessed; its light absorbed
by fibrous layers.
These things for which I claim
no responsibility
persist in making demands,
response taking profit
from such attention.
The door closes quietly
on all that has passed
at any given moment.

The News

The events are sensational and continuous,
unlike my cold feet below the table.
A letter informs me of what was said
with several tightly spaced lines;
a rush of syntax.
My shoes are threadbare and falling apart,
an elegy to footwear.
The signature implies further knowledge;
contact suspended rather than expired.
Whereas, precise and otherwise,
the news labours on
adding postscript after postscript,
beyond the range of the shoes, their contents,
this letter, its information,
and the indefatigable index
of what has yet to occur.

                                                  4 JANUARY 1973

Mist loiters throughout the afternoon
Snagged up on trees
Flopped loosely in hollows
You decide to go out for a walk
To change your mind
The sun does not appear
And then it does and sets

5 JANUARY 1973

Sitting on the Sidelines

Now it seems that all our efforts led back,
that the excursion returned us to our real lives,
with their inimitable changes,
some less acceptable than others,
but removed far enough from the originals
to be admitted,
through which absence has determined
a method of approaching the commonplace
with courtesy, with a little respect,
with considerable awe.

And the subtle overtones offered by the season;
apple trees stripped of their foliage,
with perished fruit suspended still, and intact
despite rain and wind harassments.
A puzzle to harvest logic,
the hand withheld,
first by absence, now by lack of motive,
and the greater more pressing demands
of familiar objects we address and know.

The view from the window
dilates the fluid stages of first light,
the handsome and compelling hours
where birds forage and invent a sky
in the filigree of tangled shrubs,
and the wind moulds a ragged shift of clouds,
reversing the dun layers of a rain drenched morning.
I watch, sitting at the window, absently jotting.

25 NOVEMBER 1974

the bowl of marigolds on the cabinet
asserts itself by being
and begins the unmasking of deceptions

the yellow and the water
exchange crisp signals
one to the other in vivid smears

ten minutes have passed
and I am no longer part of their exactness

a procession of indifferences
encapsulated in the confrontation
is consumed by a forgetfulness
usually reserved to deal with
the loss of treasured relics

the missing items
being like flowers in water
of a reciprocal nature
to the expression achieved
by their absence
that expires with a gasp

                          31 DECEMBER 1972–5 MARCH 1975

Who remains to recall such afternoons
Cramped by enquiry and dubious solitude
Adrift in a woodland speculation as though searching
But for what
An indication perhaps
Or searing burst of perception
The very idea is quite enough of that

The day is absorbed by days to come
And you are impatient in a way that reminds you
Of the future, as now those times present
A calm, though obviously inexact, and probably misguided
Face that is the past

Over there a distinction
Defined because it is what you particularly notice
Trees adorn the territory of their investment
This presents itself as part now and part invention
Like going out of your way to meet yourself
And then not knowing what to say

And that old nervousness again, amplified by your desire
To mention spaces
Those filled out by summer's blooms
And certain early mornings, damp, still and ready
And that abstract notion of space implied
By these recollections
That underlies all purpose and encompasses tense
As it occurs here, dealing with matters that have passed
Beyond themselves, in order that we might reconsider
The permutations set in motion

Perhaps to deter the stark swipe
That awaits the particular argument you, and you alone
Have become familiar with

Although its mark is upon many
Indelible and suggestive of their struggle with logic
For a solution that is bright and vibrant
Exhausting as a saturday night
When all else forgotten, the town breaks off
From a week of juggling cause and effect
And shouts of laughter rattle along the streets
Awakening scenes for brief enactment
That linger in the dormant glances pressed into
Another morning another day

20 MAY 1975

the surrounding area prepares itself
summer lifts over our heads
like an unrehearsed speech
here again
chorused from ascending flashes

milky light polishes
the ornaments of pretence
removing the matter of degrees
of this and thatness
of yes we do and no we can't

to forget and continue
as though nothing has happened

and now we all feel changed
by what we have achieved
it is the reassuring knowledge
that we are alone

that the ordeal of listening
for the echo
will be a manageable chore

the frequent but distracted
cheerful though singular

fade away of its cleansing tone

12 JUNE 1975

Incredible Vistas

1

it was summer and thoughtfully calm
all gesture appeared stilled, superficial
at the corner of a green area the wavy line
descending across white, betrayed the stroke
claiming this mark as a forfeit for indiscretion
where harmony and history contrive
to assemble and dispatch their messages

2

the same wrist wearing a different time
protrudes from a fraying cuff
the hand sets out to relieve and relive
a burden of misplaced ideals
lifting the curtain that risks the tremor
of a drenching gush as rain peels back
a racing layer exposed by an immodest
and explicit sky sprawled wilfully and wide

3

the elbows of the age wear thin
and what we have learned celebrates our confusion
for we are sensibly rising to the occasion
as it seeks out what remains of our vanity
because it is here, in this room
whose window reveals the distortion
of an invented view that retreats
we settle for the renewal of risk

25 JUNE 1975

Sun House Propaganda

The hot june days of august push
their advantage to the limits of public opinion
rising through the eighties in banner headlines

An embossed footpath slopes persuasively
from the flimsy shade of summer foliage
flanked by dry lawns scuffed and dull as old shoes

The day opens all its windows
into the thick of things

Abandoned deck chairs sag over smudged shadows
in cohesive light and dusty layers
that deceive the eye

And all those matters thought devious or complex
pause for a while and then dissolve
leaving a muddle of anxious reflections

About to move again
the air shakes out a specious drumming
pressing furrows into the emulsified surface
of the ornamental pond with a shrug
and the mind you change retains the thought
of water in a glass fogged by condensation
heading for the sun

Distorting the line of least resistance
the line you read
to verify the hazard of present events

9 AUGUST 1975

The Preparations

Now it is almost too late it is time for a beginning
Now it is closer to the reason for itself

Day by day our attention is repaid in particulars
But the afternoon, that is about to close for the day

The result of imagination stumbling around
Looking for a way out at the crucial moment

The edges of damp leaves curl in the drying wind
Forming tiny green fists that beat the air resentfully

Part of another situation that seems to delight in evading
Your approach, your attitude to this portion of your life

That alters, like a cake, reduced by each bite
And is an example of erratic reductions of the panorama

Generations are assured of their future labours
And are acquainted with this knowledge telepathically

But that is nothing, you hear a some-one proclaim
And they are right, in the way that plugging a gap in the view

Maybe is constructive, qualifies for praise, encouragement
A suitably composed dedication, a promissory note

A new theory of language and communication
To explain the details in full and splendid accuracy

But there are conditions, and knowing the nature of deceit
Excuse me; defeat, the state of mind may be to relax

To succumb to the announcement that this is done
With scrupulous attention to names and the dates they inhabit

The strength of our ardour as we fidget between the lines
The quixotic delight with which we anticipate the next move

                          20 AUGUST 1975

All the alternatives unite and place their complex proposal
before me, before breakfast; and lately after dinner too.
Much as I would like it otherwise this explains little;
perhaps the air loses its components, the day passes
into the filled page unrecognised; perhaps it is here
and you can't relate, may be elsewhere and you are spending
too much time on a diagnosis, and whatever else may serve
as participant in what that might mean. Meanwhile
a makeshift supper digests in the warm dark pocket
behind your belt, if you wear one, and nothing much
else seems likely to propose itself at this timid hour.
But stubbornly I persist, reaching for a Collected Works,
intent on discovering the secret of its outward gesture,
as one might set about solving a fabulous equation
in spite of the odds against such an interpretation.
But death claims a commission and a subtraction,
and no use the surprised, 'how did that get in here?', look.
The lost field of your gaze broken dimly by fractions
gathers all the false hopes and places them here, out of nowhere,
the empty room swarming with perfect answers, expected
and amazed, a delight to the ears, belonging without exception
to the questions proposed, but by some other, not you.
Today again, and the sun on leaves, departing from gentle air
as the sky swells out of itself, growing lighter and lighter,
until it is dark, and seems to touch you, but never can
make contact, although you furnish it with an inspired smile;
like the sun spills something grey with yellow stains, then pink,
and slow and palest green, knowing the way the air settles
into fragile shades, no-one else around to notice at this hour,
then blue, applied in translucent laminae,
above the day established

27 OCTOBER 1975

Exercise for One Leg

the window is left open
and it does not matter
outside rushes in
with no curtain to gesture
at the passing
I am glad although my mood will not admit it
I want to ask you questions
but I am not around to receive the answers
I am in here dancing on one leg
as my rhythm gradually escapes the music
first to be heard
then to be silent
though my foot keeps time
it is after all only a gesture of desire
the music has outlasted my requirement
the pain above my left eye reaches out
to a hint of green
where new shoots follow mapped light
how else can one evaluate the product
of three months editing one's feelings
when sleeplessness recedes
as the night crawls back from dawn
and each word stands in profile
defining space exchanging surroundings
with heartening determination
and the tropic light sweeps and changes
as the source reacts
rising towards its zenith
on a glorious arc that traces my need

26 MARCH 1976

Occupying Absence

Low cloud rides the lure
of light to moderate southerlies
then it goes up very high opens and fills
the collective eye
now I'm back here again
have returned to taste the pages
torn from the book
where once it was february 1974
back here again as I said
simply by turning the pages
and avoiding the in between

It was pleasant for a time
to jump clear
to know that and miss the point
to trick the dates and choose my day
what is missing now is salted peanuts
with my wedge of cheese and glass of wine
but things do get upset so easily
the glass if I don't watch my right arm
sliding along leaving a track of words
across the sheet as if they belong there

Earlier I watered the plants
without a word of encouragement
to assist their leafy expansions
and I am in love with you
where you are which is not here
beside me as I am beside myself
in the present condition being alone
among the familiar trappings of my life

The darkness is primed and thoroughly dappled
with the variousness of its presence about us
it is as though the clear air
laden with the darkest of blues
swallows the dream I stifle with a yawn
as I finish wiping the dishes
before I relax and move on
maybe to the bookshelf or maybe to bed

          20 April 1976

January

The images are transposed
by the success of incidental mannerisms.
Snow collides with the window, bearing
symmetrical fragments of ice. The postman
walks away from the door with music
intermittently escaping from the radio
tucked behind his belt.
He figures large in a predominance of slushy grey,
eclipsed by his purpose and a prospect
of manipulative contact. The air returns
your attention with foggy breath etched
onto a window. An evergreen aroused
from temporary stupor shakes the blueness
of its green foliage against white sky. It falls,
like a fleeting glance, across the view.
The discreet nudge of the weather
answering your look. Visitors fill the room
with their intentions, with their absence,
with subdued indecision. Lavish diversions gratify
their present state, although they were thought
to be the point of their pretence.

The light shimmers theatrically,
a mannerism incidental to success, transposing
images. Opinions collide. Letters fall through
the air, propelled by a distant touch.
Instinct tears the flap, unfolds the white page,
senses the sun pressing through a dripping mask,
adjusts to a discreet reference to spring.
The colour of the day proposes certain responses.
A slight shift negotiates the immediate fear,
although I am assured more by the blank events

of tomorrow that outreach themselves. than by the
articulated procession of this expanding condition.
But the moment passes, the impulse is gratified
by a further break in the weather, a cheering
glimpse of rinsed blue. I prepare to walk to the park,
leaving the line as I enter it into the combination
of messages, which will remain until I return,
refreshed by the dilemma of finding confusion to be
a state of absence, though only in the particular.

JANUARY 77

Deliberate Modulations

The light retreats through houses
where some windows appear like postage stamps,
the commemorative type, placed on end, the image
casually erased to a point when the colours merge.
Other windows are blocked out darkly
in a kind of self denial, as though nothing has ever happened
there, until today, when vague movements tantalize
the abstractions from which such manifestations
have arisen.

All the planned and all the spontaneous gathered
as a group, each with its own back to turn, not
for the first time, or the last time, but every time
once too often.

A tissue of darkness to disguise the truth,
the vacant wind passing its hand across your eyes,
leaves moving in a bland generality
of motion, a faint dilation of light
that confirms distance on an ascending scale,
the taste it deposits when you turn to the day's business.
The question is a splendid example
for the intellect, the dealer glances across the table,
assessing degrees of strain. The wrappings are discarded
carelessly, and float in that manner, coming to rest
elsewhere, as birds swoop like a proverb
onto drowsy lawns.

This way of tracing the reckless course, defined by
pastel buntings, stacks its ruthless obstacles against
a fading impression of starless changes. To identify
and refrain from making contact, to mention the manner

in which the light dilates, delivering the next remark,
listening to each word as it passes between your teeth,
changing the substance of air with each suck and blow,
challenging the pages with each turn, as they settle back
and you prepare for action.

5 FEBRUARY 1977

Personal Choice

At first glance it appears colourless

Then your voice, identified by another
and the yellowed air fills in the details
replacing the opening words
with thunder that obliterates
their formal proposal, behind a grey muslin
of inevitable rainfall

The field of vision is enmeshed, its challenge
stunned by a rebuke
from the towering perimeter
poised above the rooftops and dead elms

Your words transcribed from magnetic tape
in to the earpiece of personal choice

As sight equates each lightning spasm
to a breath
that satisfies the blood
and ritual techniques glimpsed
through the window each word opens
focus on the mood beyond

Later when I listen
examining values, assessing proposals
all intrusive movement is fixed
in a rinsed out sunset

and I am away in the back of too much silence
working to catch a thrown voice
watching how a surface reveals the exactness

of what lies beneath
waiting to move aside for
the green and the blue, the violet and the bronze

                                    24 FEBRUARY 1977

There is no prior indication
that what has yet to reveal itself
will
until our eyes, used to the light
acquaint us with the materials

The source expands and rises
intensifying the blue of its destination
and the once white walls
glow accordingly

With nothing less than perfect balance
the present need contributes
to the aspirations of all waking hours

The white sky . . .
Along the road . . .
Simplicity that rages ahead . . .

But they too are not sufficient
Sheets of air break and move as in a dream
whose moment of waking retains that doubt
for which the answer is unclaimed

The voice complains against itself
One minute cheers and free associations
the next a closing in of substitutes
denying choice

And what advice is offered
Some days are full of chairs, longing,
uncomfortable refrains
Today excludes yesterday
Tomorrow, who can remember

5 MARCH 1977

Cold Front

Because I shiver I persuade myself,
Encapsulated by diminished body warmth,
That this spiteful cold harbours a purpose.
The rooms are bleak but adamant, absorbed
By shrinking light, like a platform
Where shadowy performers parade into the space
Remaining, enthralled by the potency emanating
From their various attributes.
One outlines the new era from a modest position
Of humourless sincerity, another rejoices,
Lacking the simple anchorage of a pertinent occasion.
Part of the scenery burns with a halo of misted light.
You suspect this pause might amplify
A general reduction in the levels of concentration.
Preoccupied by the timetable for the day's journey,
You fail to witness the sense of refreshed air
Blowing through the open door, but it is
Really only that blast catching at your ankles,
Above the line of your new wool socks.
A shiver does it! and you are on the move,
To coat, gloves, and scarf; the knock at the door,
The ride to the airport, out and up through swirls
Of morning fog in pressurised flight.
Twenty-two pages later is touchdown,
And early morning confusion has been forgotten
In the state of half sleep and half wakefulness,
Depending on which direction you are coming from.
Now there is an interval, over macaroni and cheese
With green salad, for eavesdropping adjacent conversations.
But that proves unsatisfactory, although at least
There is nothing much to fool you, except perhaps
Your own persistence in searching for light relief.
And now that is all behind you, the retreating day
Gathers in the windows that frame dissolving views,
And block the cold front that, like a cartilaginous rind,

Circumscribes the platinum moon.
But now it is warm again and I am in danger of falling
Asleep with this book in my hands, the place marker
On the floor, and the light burning vacantly
Behind my head. The problem is, will the last line
Be read or written, and how will I tell you which?

16 NOVEMBER 1977

Vital Matters

A ray pierces dissolving vapour
yellowing the walls with retouched light,
and a patina effect that numbs
the adjectives' reaction to its presence,
resisting effort that loads the matter,
now annexed in a moment of relief.

Much of the marginal jotting
has been obliterated; of those words remaining
on the field, the following are legible:
"Resisting arrest", "Loaded", "Vital matters.
Name them", "We are that same person, you and I".
No longer a key to anything but their own existence,
cancelling any last instructions, they poise
artfully, unable to plunge from the tableau,
too late in the day and delayed.

Grown out of itself, this same lateness assumes
a timeless contracting, dispersed through channels
and shadows. So what has been accumulated in
the shifting interval of gradations,
seems to prevent the policy getting out of hand.
Attention adjusts in such a way
that earlier conjecture becomes a reliable source
for accurate debate. The spectacle is eclipsed
by what now remains of the evidence,
all that we have and all that we are to witness.

"We are I, you, and that same person", "Vital arrest.
Resisting matters", "Name them", "Loaded".
Retouched with adjectives the tableau dissolves,
its marginal existence yellowing in artful delays.
The day plunges, in a moment of anything but poise,
from the pierced walls.
Cancelling themselves, the words instruct the field

arrayed with yellowing vapours, resist the patina effect
that numbs, strike out what has been obliterated,
renew the moment.

By these manipulative steps the surrounding conventions
materialise from that disguise, casting wigs, garments
and postures to the ground.
The evidence is witnessed and eclipsed,
and we remain to carry on.

7 SEPTEMBER 1977–21 JANUARY 1978

Theory

Awake between times and now
it is later, out in the streets
breathing common air
spiced with an abundance of exhalations.
Voices adjoining distort the silence
of events following a spiral
firmly located in the after hours.
One of the pleasures of our days
hisses to a stop.
Low altitude cover rolls
back across the allotments off
the fire-station tower,
away from the white clock
tower of the garage, decked out
with red neon letters and border
outlines, off the fuzz of trees,
up and over my head replaced
by an evening blue fade.
Now we are irritable and vicious,
part of another occasion
that circumscribes the subjectivity
of a mirror. That worth equated with
striving results in satisfactory
solutions, is a popular misconception
seen repeatedly where barren wastes
deny their own proliferation, in arriving
at nothing but the familiar trappings
of achievement.

14 SEPTEMBER 1977–21 JANUARY 1978

Bulletin

Turn the page and read
the view there, stunned
by tactics of recall, and how
they arrange themselves. Wanting
to be there, and when there,
restless with the need to alter
the pattern.
Today feels like that,
reduced by fits and starts,
gathered to the limits
of the foreseeable future.
The afternoon is moody but approachable.
A sudden shower obliterates
last remnants of light. No,
not our adversaries, who don't
possess such influence,
but inclement weather, to which they bear
a marked resemblance.
The implications are many and various
as is the news, withholding one truth
in favour of another.
In here the air is cooler, and the coffee
warmer, and a deed defeats a word
when all that was required of it
slips away into the distortion
of events glossed over by the working day,
supporting a routine from which we retreat
cancelling numbers, covering our tracks,
travelling through borrowed time.

SEPTEMBER 1977–22 JANUARY 1978

Best Foot

Like that same day worn smooth by storms
the subject receded,
its tricky but unerring changes
obliterate a non-event.

Proposals and questions, you may remember
how it began with the elimination
of each hour, as though that chance
to divulge such intelligence
would never pass you by again.

Need is an over generous definition of
the condition, the subsequent encircling
of facts and obsequious rhetoric.

The Indian summer fills what remains
of the season, dressed in side-shows, stalls
and minor calamities, that will be reduced
by further comparison.

Now we are here, and across your shoulder
the sun illuminates the morning after feeling
with an innocent look, unmasks a window
to the gaping sky and slides behind
a silhouette of warehouses.

You press the text of your hands
onto the Indian air, the signs are altered
and the purpose of the hour retreats.
The fingers instruct their region
to appear on command, and with best foot
forward you negotiate the changes
towards where I believe I stand.

30 AUGUST 1977–21 JANUARY 1978

Mixed Feelings

Alarm pulls at my sleeve
like a worsening climate. The explicit wind
flattens fences, tosses shrubbery to a blur,
strips roofs of their cladding,
is treacherous but compelling
with its extravagances and passing
strange disclosures.
Hopeless light traverses the lop-sided afternoon.
I trace its course by a diminishing wake,
then apply my attention to the proposition
up ahead.
Then I am free to leave
with nowhere particular to go. Traces
of anxiety. Tracers of false witness.
Reckless air conflicts with this resolve,
confronts the conclusion, gathers momentum
and debris, and admits to a preference
for enigmatic jollification,
instamatic recording of events, pneumatic
methods of judgement.
The present disreputable crowd
have been counted in, and seduce the non-existent
present with a compelling account of the future,
with true reason, a precise and clear vision
allied to a certain elusiveness of personality.
We communicate these basic factors,
together with our excesses and failings,
that filter the incessant contradictions
of our strategies. We pause for refreshment,
sans suspicious glances, developing a method
for discovering all the undisclosed secrets
of clever works, and find there are none.

But the question that follows is re-routed
by the vital shift in provocation and
the prevailing mood of those who stay.

                28 August 1977–21 January 1978

Just Deserts

The morning's mask of cool
moist light ascends
to modernist blue, meshed by green.

Shards and particles and words
press down and forwards
like a best foot. The sense
of their capability materializes
from the thin air undiluted.
Praise be to the continuing
independence of language.

And whoever says labour is noble
when not a constant delight,
or imbued with glorious velocity,
deserves a kick in the head.

Resentment of particulars
is a cargo jettisoned in the wake
of the advance. Returning possesses
no value, except to nudge the edge
of some thing we recall
from the vantage point of here
and now.

And now it is raining,
with a gentle hiss, through
tall grass and stiffening leaves.

The sun appears when least expected,
shedding explanatory light
on the letter abandoned mid
sentence. Even the clearing sky,
ransacked by testy air,
interrogates the secretive reckoning

by which the transactions are reviewed
and marked accordingly.

And marked accordingly the quickened
stroke abuses preferential choice.

1 MAY 1978

Mooning

The realm of a dedicated practitioner
Expands perversely by virtue

Of its density, but will never be
Unimpeachable, though his timely withdrawal

From membership of the personality cult
May be construed as an attribute,

Or may not be any such sacrifice
If mooning over the extraordinary disorder

Of representation distorts the agility
And inveterate habit of conspicuous

Observation. The day requests the pleasure
Of your company, flutters to a pre-set signal

Adjusting the view to a most appealing angle.

A claim for renewed vitality is without
Dignity, weather permitting request a little

More time, and who needs that kind of dignity
Anyway, not to be confused with elaborate fragments

From a ritualised continuity employed by
Rationalists. The addition of variants in this

Remark repudiated once more
By an immense infusion of light.

You cannot be accounted for. Your alibi
Is true to the known facts,

Which convey an awful between the lines
Sentiment of latent exultation dismantled.

16 August 1978

Recipe

The ingredients are vicious
But fitting

The climate is varied and enduring
Intent on image manipulation
Endorsed by self interest
That delivers a common wish
To survive

Rain falls out of context
Onto the fabric we generally disregard
Can it be that we are avoiding
The products of a hostile claim
Now resentful of times past caring
Now happy to depart on a visit

Why are we still hanging around
So long after the street corner
Was demolished
Sharpening our blades and our wits
On any raw material that is convenient

We recall the words and the tune
And repeat the song
Until it is truly forgotten

AUGUST 1978

Shorts Garden

It is lunch time,
and I do not hesitate to look
over my shoulder once
at the passersby.

In energetic but transitory contact
with intellect, and my purpose.

The thought of recognising power
and weakness, those necessary limits
to the choice of food,

its vast range,
no quarrel.

Suppose that between intellect and spirit,
thought and faith,
the relationship was not one of perfect
harmony, what then?
There are unmistakable traces
of human nature at its most purposeful
and independent here.

The ally and discoverer of truth
disputes such claims and revelations,
even though my solitary exercise
is diverted into your path.

The guardian of the fall is acting
under orders. Thank you for your timely
interruption.

For instance, we do not say to ourselves,
again and again, we suspect nothing.
Arrogant pretensions speak less truly
of such attitudes.

Just as you speak to me
and I read that dogma challenges free will.

And we walk away together
in separate directions.

SEPTEMBER 1978

Incredible Vistas 2

1

Preparations have a way of confusing intentions.
How like you, their adverse effects unravelling
such a disorderly profile. A twist of light,
a nudge in the ribs, an upstart preamble.
All variables and combinations mentioned in one
fraudulent breath. The collective influence
mobilised in the wake of terminological subterfuge.

2

The street map is unencumbered by personal choice.
The dead are masters of their own outrageous destiny,
ignoring the clamour for retrospective devices.
In this peculiar outbuilding there is no sense
of passion. And there is no radio. The darkness
over the fens gives a sharper edge to daylight,
and when it returns we do not know which way round
or how to get out, but try even harder.

3

The white china cup and saucer are rimmed with gold,
and flawed. Red roses fester in sludge deposits
in the cup, courtesy of Dairy Crest Milk. In the base
of the ashtray a gross and corpulent cherub lolls
between urns and cigarette ends. I'd like a hangover
for the morning, but all I'll get is an early call.

DECEMBER 1978

Now and Then
for John Riley

According to the impeccable calibrations
of my Boots Diary, nineteen seventy two edition,
the month in question was July, the day
was saturday, and I am doing my utmost
to remember, now you are not here to respond
and your last letter requires no answer,
which is what this is.
The weather was too warm for comfort,
unlike that is today,
which bears resplendent
your inimitable style despite the fog
that fails to obscure the essential process
as it burns away the rigmarole from meaning.
That evening never was completed
to our satisfaction.
Now it is late, according to the not so impeccable
calibrations on my wrist-watch dial,
and the air outside carries itself
aloof and cold through combinations of time
and place, searching the narrative
for a simple and provoking epigraph.
Wednesday is the day in question
as tomorrow approaches and the light
recedes, constant and rational;
will serve the purpose,
in the hope that nothing will be forgotten,
that no part will be ignored, and that
the thoughts of the few will encourage
the recall of many to your
"sixth sense
              of the invisible"
whose progress continues
beyond us all.

10/22 January 1979

Airs and Graces

March airs itself and
graces the sky.
Jackets off, we flex our rate
of endurance.

The surroundings retain their
anonymity, decked out in winter drab,
withholding co-operation for
a better offer. It is deserved,
and should be equal to this blue expanse
we have stopped to admire
when no one else is looking.

There are many words in the freshly
exposed prospect,
where the general idea assumes control,
placing a hand on the arm,
a foot in the door,
a variable in the specific.
Rudimentary polemics, like the national
debt, have a hand in my pocket,
and it's fondling my balls.

At least it's not raining.
The general idea removes its uniform,
there is no question to compare
with this exposure.
The absence of imponderables.
The curious glances of the exploiters.

Then there is the horizon,
too far away again, what's needed here
is a closer look at the power complex.
A curious manifestation in the weak
link of the system.

Cold shrug, icy regard,
blustering mismanagement,
feeble justifications.

The watermeadows are awash.
Banks are breached,
byelaws are bypassed,
restrictions are lifted
and the facts seep out
staining the numbed and collapsing sky.

                                                   7 MARCH 1979

So What!

Waking in the afternoon
is a rare pleasure, the air
a degree or so too cool for comfort
and the light erring on the gaudy side,
too much saffron
through the verdant mottle in the yard.
For little more time than it takes
to fill a kettle,
the day seems at a loss, backing
away hastily from the display
of sluggish stirring.
But you know
that it is merely a trick of the eye,
certainly not to be attributed to
this blasé edge of the hour,
in search of a word or two
in lieu of guessing who
spoke out, what comment would manage
a contradiction of the chafing breeze
preceding this stormy hustle.
So what
a time to think about tomorrow
as raw material, I like
the strategy of the outline,
and for as long as it's imminent
keep at it.
Waking is a rare pleasure,
an elaborate resilience to what
will attract your attention
by default.

28 APRIL 1979

Inspiration is Just a Guy Called Art

Recently I read, "pain is a great incentive
to art."
Which proves two things;
I've been reading again,
and you can not trust the printed word
until you have experienced that which it proposes.
Meanwhile treat it like it does not exist.

Pain is a great incentive,
but present understanding suggests
that it prevents more than is promised,
rather than being prelude
to a blinding exposure to insight and wisdom.

We should be thankful that the age of innocence
will never exist, dreamed by confectioners.
Do not get in the way of too much
spongey optimism, a sure hazard of the repressive kind.
Two jumps ahead,
so look what reading has done for us,
cutely gliding
over and beyond the obstacle.

But no easy landing, although daily training
prevents a complete breakdown of the balance mechanism.
Standing here,
two feet diverting from an intended course, free
to speculate on surrounding productions of serious air.

All the time in the world,
who counts the minutes spends the hours extravagantly.
The attractions of a chance remark

put you at ease when all around
an obsessive dismantling of language
expands and vibrates like a swarm
of voracious insects, darkening the cycle
of empty light.

APRIL 1979

*"Do you love me, or are you merely extending goodwill?
I'd like to get me some of that goodwill."*

If you do
I like the tone. A voice
that works on imagination
extracting honest response.

Take another sip,
have another drag. Such social graces
usually bring out the recluse
who hides behind the folded page.

There is a preposterous certainty
assures the least expected
of a place in our hearts.
Flagging spirits seem miraculously revived,
fluttering like a turn in the weather.

The atmosphere is quite striking now,
smoother and less repelling.
I walk home in the consequent charm
of such commonplace recovery.
Clouds are reduced to a wrinkled brow
whose edges frown
at the luminous remains of the day.

I travelled to the limit
of the first half of a return ticket.
Some of the time it rained,
and some of the time I read.
Tomorrow I will tell you all about it,

this theory of reason I continue
to formulate, that constantly eludes me.
Are you extending goodwill,
or do you merely love me?

                                      16 MAY 1979

Light

At three in the morning
nothing moves. The occasional sound
emanates from my presence as I move
about making a hot drink,
setting a chair to face the window
in preparation for the coming day.

I am pleased by the light somewhere,
dawn is shaping up well;
the order of events is preconditional,
obeying a natural law,
distinct and not unlike a slight reprimand
to the incautious.

Like yesterday afternoon
seemed preposterous with people wandering
along the road,
a distant look in their eyes
that cannot be described,
nor would identify present intentions.

Eventually having overcome the problem
of evening festivities, whose allure
was like a trap of comparable ideas,
I assume control,
I am determined,
often a little previous,

and sometimes obsolete;
I share this honour, its value self-evident,
reaching the chosen (the nameless and fictitious),
by means of transfer mechanics,
their primitive intention independent
of the outstretched hand,

and its ingenious structures to which we are immune.
The audience
becomes the singular
manifestation
of its component parts,
behind the curtain,

adding a complication of chosen terms
to a complication of separate ways.
Personally I prefer that moment when
stars disappear without trace,
dazzled by surrounding materials
of crude but exquisite address.

28 MAY 1979

Testing Testing Testing

A false address will go some way

to ensure notoriety,
and avoid a destination.

Rhythms, methods, themes, devices
conjoin in the blue rinse of printer's ink.

I can feel myself becoming nasty,
I can detect a crusty edge.
Too many choices absolve their variable delights.

We deserve ourselves,
not to put too fine a point on it,
the knife slips, the lead snaps.
You deserve us too.
There is no future in memory and recall,
reasoning overtakes the mechanics of the pen.

One truth remains
refusing definition,

retaining integrity, alone
and emerging from eclectic principles.

The outlook is framed
by a hard edge of formal light.
The outlook is the substance of the day,
a collection of cheap tricks.

The day is restless with evidence
that concealis the meaning of passionate
substance. The question is waiting

for the writing to stop

           14 JUNE 1979

Talking Air

There are events that constantly evade,
or enlarge slowly, as if seen through lens glass,
the very actions approaching from some distant point
with a dust cloud clinging in their wake.
It seemed impossible but the sky
had parts of lemon yellow, mingled
with the usual colours.
And you came along
engrossed in the act of selecting a key.
Then there is the problem of making contact.
I've dialled a number that is permanently engaged,
and it is long past the time
for my departure.
The monotonous rhythm of digits reaching,
like a hand in greeting, towards you,
after I have gone.
If you answer what will I say?
Should I contemplate delay,
or complicate my position by leaving?
The colours anticipate the move,
drifting aimlessly through general light,
the hard facts of the place
are floating at eye-level like hideous cushions.
Arranged by fumbling air the brilliant light
in an elaborate but spontaneous surge
kindly blurs their obsequious presence.

JULY 1979

Hotel Zingo

Today lacks the conviction of my feelings,
and my feelings lack the heart
of the matter. The cold drink
from the vending machine
is a weak sizzling potion
of remote origin, saturated with
carbon-dioxide zest.
Enough is enough before the second sip,
in a strange country, with a different tongue.
I'm getting sick;
the light has turned a nasty and peculiar colour,
tasting of oranges and vodka.
If you arrive now I will be out
in the streets, averting my eyes, stumbling
moodily into crowded bars,
looking for a way to the future,
with a lump in my throat from too many peanuts
and too many cigarettes.
Is this a combination that will delight
the audience of contemporary verse?
And where are you?

There is something odd
about sitting in such a remote place,
curtains open to the world, wanting to be
somewhere else as though that might be
the answer, while people pass below the window,
getting on with the day and its variations
on a theme.
If I am moved I am moving now
in the prepared direction, reprieved
and curiously at ease with the travel arrangements.

My bag is packed, my bill is paid,
my foot is through the door,
and the morning air is the air you breathe
that crumbles the words I have to say
to you, when we meet.
The solid body of natural desire,
the pliable substance of disastrous thought.

                                                  5 JULY 1979

Pact and Impact

The uncomfortable facts of verisimilitude,
the malaise of miles away, the window

and the walls; again a familiar landmark,
again the evidence of living in,

of leaving out, of letting go.
The evidence of your interest as it falls,

like a clear day falls through cloud,
exposing the distant infiltration

of stunning blue. Exposing the conflagration
of personal dilemma, adorned with the real

and the imaginary products of fallibility.
The fundamental ease of a firm line

meticulously detailed, perfectly terminated,
existing within the boundaries of shrinking days.

10 SEPTEMBER 1979

The evening is falling away sharply
to another metaphor,
up in the air
and down at heel, that sparkles
for a moment, then dulled,
retreats into itself.

The mornings are colder
and later,
smudged onto the window
by the thumb of damp grey ambiguity.

The door and the decade are closing fast
with attentive but obvious comments.

Talking to myself
is no substitute for conversation,
and more often than not
I fail to reply.

Today, this particular afternoon,
carries its age remorselessly forward,
held like a banner
that snaps waspishly in the wind.

Some of the textures remind me of you,
they are not a painting,
but the visual impact is comparable
and settles alongside other
less elaborate decisions, to come to the point
in a sudden memory of brilliance
and self-containment.

6 OCTOBER 1979

Common Denominator

Momentarily aligned, the sunlight
behind the tree, outside the window,
erodes the defining edges of the leaves
that quiver and vibrate
in the tranquillized waftings of the afternoon.
The room is alive and flickering
with projected vitality.
The rooms at the back of the house
hold less appeal.
                    Street movements and noises
are reduced to a drone, a silence
that flinches apologetically,
and constant north light fails to enhance
the paraphernalia and objects of memory,
their anxieties and their elations,
the irrevocable process
of their attraction.
                  I am attracted
to them now, but they remain aloof
and engrossed in their intelligent procedures,
ignorant of, or merely ignoring,
my request for an adjournment.
                        Meanwhile,
some thoughts in passing
are caught up and absorbed
by the varied and distinguished structure.
Submission is an alternative
to my keeping a distance from such appendages
which have become, are, intrinsic
to the identity I assume as mine.

So what other course of action but to succumb,
to extrapolate on the given and available facts.
It hurts somewhere behind the scenes
where an elaborate but two-dimensional backdrop

rises slowly into the fly-tower,
revealing deeply shadowed recesses,
gantries and fragile catwalks.
My lines of communication are open to you,
without a second's thought and with first hand
news of the state of things,
here in the realms of mime
on reams of paper, marked by the common denominator
of our unknown destination.

                              24 SEPTEMBER/11 OCTOBER 1979

Here Today Here Tomorrow

It is nine o'clock where you are breakfasting,
and I have eaten a late lunch here.

The morning paper lies unread on the floor,
and the present facts of our lives are beginning
to sound like a news item. This and nausea
combine with intermittent bursts of activity
to occupy my time today.

The telephone rang twice, and each time I spoke
the receiver went dead
with a disturbing buzz and click. Who is out
there trying to make contact? Is it you?
Is it me they want to talk to anyway?
There was no answer then, there is
no answer now.

Mr Lyons calls to ask if I have any knives
that need sharpening, or scissors. I don't,
I am indisposed, they are in the drawer
dulled by boredom. I give him some cigarettes
and money, and he leaves feigning satisfaction,
wishing me luck.

I return to the work in hand, it is taking shape
like a knife,
but it is in my back.

16 OCTOBER 1979

Flying

Daylight is pared
by seasonal changes, much as life is
by personal ones.
The clouds have drifted into a ruck
between identical blues
of the sea and the sky.
The lower blue is flecked with white
on a surface of what appears,
at closer examination, to be
a two tone ground.
The inevitable sunlight is bright
and unforgiving, although the unforgiving
part is regularly modified
during the twenty-four hours cycle
that the globe rides with such aplomb.

Falling asleep can be pleasant, but waking,
especially to the jolt of turbulence
and disorientation, is often accompanied
by the cold and creepy realisation
that you are still up there, up in the air
that is, and coming down fast.
Most times these sensations are quickly adjusted
and accepted as inevitable,
dependence being placed on the miracles
of technology, and the pilot's competence
in manipulating same.

Seeing the earth translated,
like a small scale map printed on
absorbent paper, is both delightful and
informative to the receptive eye.

If the day is overcast the view is abstract,
and sometimes vice versa.
All geography and art lessons
should be conducted at one thousand feet.

It is also possible to sense the ultimate
isolation while sitting shoulder to shoulder
with one's fellows.
An emotion that is disconcerting and reassuring
without losing integrity.
Landing is always an uncompromising relief,
and a renewed investment in the art of self
motivation. The journey is continuous
and forward, and the destination here and now.

21 August/17 October 1979

Post Script

The knowledge of your whereabouts
is tempered by the absence
of an exact location.

When the air moves against me
it is not you, and I roll down
my shirt sleeves anticipating
further chill.

From a sky stripped of variables
grey light tilts at the window.
Some darker shadows intrude
to accumulate in layers
slanted to the light,
minute by minute consumed
by the deepening fascia of the night.

These are some of the events
arising from the past hours,
and the sound of last night's rain
pestering the roof, lingers in my head.

For those of us who remain
attending to the vigil
of our dubious art, the reward is
the fun of finding the morning
up and about before us,
even though we resisted sleep
to fabricate this accomplishment.

And we remain here,
completing the task, stumbling
to the bathroom to attend to
the final revisions, the reparation of sleep,
before we meet again
in the future tense of our accessibility.

                      17 JULY/19 OCTOBER 1979

Trans (1989)

Address

It is not enough to know the time,
one has to be there.
Hello then.

It was Orion, that star
formation. It was Ursa Minor
and a star cluster.
It was nothing
but the night sky expanding
with a distant hum
above our upturned heads.
The meteor, short and splendid,
scored a diagonal line, returning
to dust.
One of us did not see
and we're not saying who.

There is an answer
but you are looking uneasy
and I am looking at you,
before we look away.

The stars continue through the night
and fade in our wake
as we pass beneath them
to fade into sleep,
no final question asked,
no answer finally given.

Double Take 1

Deliberation as a form
of rebuke.

With no time like the present you prepare
to receive
the final, irrefutable worthlessness.
Something of a catch

phrase, you are breathing deep and even.
Relaxed in a monotony
that outweighs any proposal
of disruptive activity
during the displacement of hours.
The cold night's pragmatic wish
for corrective adjustment.

For dawn to congratulate
in an act of partition.
The senses that demand the highest price,
with no profit, no margin
for error,
no risk but total commitment,
no whimsical flexibility
but real articulation.

The relentless indulgence
of an answer.

If it fits, wear its language
like a glove
to the cheek of adversity.

Double Take 2

The rim of the eyelid
closes like an awning to protect
the eyeball
from the scrutiny of the sun.

A symptom
of what curious malaise?

In early light
I watch the murky view
emerge from translucent fog
into a solemn and flimsy cartoon
of the real

Getting up early
can still prove to be too late,
with determination and enthusiasm
stumbling as a pair
out into the bland light
as though the summit of such achievement
had been conquered at a stroke.

As though the legacy of such losses
can accommodate such gains.
Progression has that quality
most difficult to apply.

I had an Uncle
who used a horse's gall-stone
as a paper weight,
his pens lay on a marble stand,
its ink well was invariably dry.
They are both dead now,
although the deliberations of memory
continue to restate

and employ their passing.
as though their summit
was a higher plane that they had reached
with a faintly mocking gaze,
an impudent aside
to the blank page of their demise.

Trans

I give my name at the enquiry window. They check the list, repeat it, mark a
form ask me to sit and lift the telephone to say I have arrived. I have
arrived, the page confirms this fact.
By the door a mother and daughter talk quietly. The mother is explaining
that she is about to leave, detailing the reasons for her departure. addressing
the inclined and averted face of the girl. Her silence, the girl's, a troubled
accusation, is impossible to ignore. Words I fail to hear, spoken for my
benefit only, privacy and exclusion. I turn my back to the door to place them
out of range. Now I can see you walking along the corridor. For a moment I
forget and they have gone, you are still there and closer and I stand to greet
you face to face.

A woman steps between us to ask me for a light for her cigarette.

A man weeps quietly in a corner. A cooling breeze blows through the doors.

The counter clerk allocates a room number and I hand over my box of
matches. At times like this, times like this seem a little absurd. Times like this
are all too common. We sit, you smile, I ask you, how does one get out of
here? You point to the door, and say, there. Tell me what you are thinking

Tell me exactly what you are thinking. I think about the door,
	walking along
the corridor, across the car park, down the road, away, at times
	like this. You
are looking at me looking at the tree outside the window. I say I
	am thinking
about the tranquility of this room. I say, the same time next
	week. We say
goodbye at the door. The sky has broken into massive clouds.

Revisions
for Douglas Oliver

His attention is distracted
to a slight movement in one of the lower apertures.

When to act and when to remain inert. These are just two of the
questions we will be dealing with this evening.

The elevations are transmitters of spatial geometry. Holes to
let in the light and holes through which to enter and leave.

No art taboo and no grand gesture can eliminate the poignancy of
such devices.

Between the buildings the action is meticulously executed, all moves
perfectly synchronised.

Reason my dears, is not consulted.

There is an expression of force for which no symbol yet exists.

I was looking for something that reminded me of what I
said to you in a recent letter. Postscript to action.

Nudge a righteous citizen's sensibilities.

The street is filled with debris and daybreak. Broken glass
on the pavement mocks hysterical destruction but will not
relinquish that state.

A figure breaks from cover and runs, crouching low, into
the shadow of a doorway.

The element of surprise makes hostages of us all.

Playback

1

Numerous complicities
reward curiosity with a smirk.
Occasional furniture fails to reveal
any other function.
No further information.

No further information
is neither here nor there.

You cannot sit in the word chair.
Your imagination can, and it is
the thought that counts.

I remember the smell of Brylcreem
in my father's hat.

2

Anything could happen
and nothing does.

No one arrives.

Such elaborate dispossession
goes unremarked.
and no one arrives.

Yearning silence at odds
with yawning response.

Living with danger,
anything could happen.
It is the danger of the unrehearsed.
manœuvring with difficulty.

3

Casual lives conduct their ways like illustrated articles
about distant places. All the names are unusual but appropriate.
One is called away on a matter requiring immediate attention.
Another is called away to attend to invisible assets.
Who can say who will be next. Response by conditioning. Layers
    of congested
air distribute brittle static across the sky's former shape.

4

Will the main event demand?
Have the lines rejoined, is the intersection
clear? Has it stopped, is it making
no headway?
Is this contradiction out of control?
This vessel, this event?

Repeat request.

Will the particular encourage
sustained concentration?

Repeat request.
Prepare an order of deletions.

Oceans circumscribe the land
fish float in water, the air churns,
squalls rejoice in participations
of this type. Roads run tricky courses.
We all know a hard bargain
when it hits us in the teeth.

5

Ornaments of regret
and atrocious adornment
glitter in unstable light.

Who is disturbed?
What risks?

6

Nothing is the same as little has changed.
As a summary of daily events proves.
Running into danger where it presently resides.

It would be impossible to mistake your whereabouts.
Where are you?
Nothing is the same before it changes.

7

To fabricate a plan
against bewilderment.

Nothing doing!

Wardrobes in three locations,
has unhealthy connotations.

With your eyes shut the pattern alters.
This then repeated on the retina.
Then this.
A bewildering structure of intentions.
A rainy day in summer.
Surfaces looped with threads of light.
Roaming the streets of commonplace.

8

Feet are the serifs
of the body.

The absent minded host
steps into every toe-hold,

scaling the steep pitch of recognition.

A question is tolerated if its statuesque form
compliments the ground he walks on.

When he turns, it is too late to see
who has already departed.

9

It would appear
that all is not
what it seems.

Stating the obvious,
obviously.

It seems that all is not
what it would appear
to be.

This has nothing to do
with what I am saying,

but it is a truth,
and it does deny
the obvious.

10

Determined air strap-hangs from the eaves.
Events catch you unawares, erasing a state

of revisionist ceremony.
The wind is deliberately brief.

A smile of bogus delight varies but little.
Avoiding the face, the unpredictable

anniversaries celebrated there.

Instructions as an art form.

If you have heard them once, you have
heard them, deliberately brief and incidental.

If you tell yourself, No Choice, you are lost.
Get out and do something brave and frivolous,

it is not yet the end of the world,
though only just.

Rain

The rain stopped the clouds dissolved
the sun set in cool peach undemanding blue
and horrid orange. The wet pavements dried,
leaving pools of sparkling water,
bright and snappy as pain.
The taxi was abandoned.
The way back was abandoned. Poor light
abandoned the street, poor visibility
assumed control. The circuit was interrupted,
contact broken.

Expressions of regret were abandoned. The next
day was abandoned. The past was passed
and abandoned to a non-aligned future.
A careless detour to avoid care.

The Northern Line was abandoned. The seven minute
walk and the flying ants were abandoned.
The sticky leaves and low branches
of the lime trees were abandoned.
The corporate web was abandoned, together
with the basic understanding of most forms
of communication and response.

The books, papers and green typewriter,
were abandoned. The effects and affects
of post-modernist theories and manipulations,

the letters arriving, and the letters
departing, the phone calls and invitations,
abandoned.
The cloak and dagger of intention abandoned.
The make-shift make-up department, smudged
and smeared, and abandoned. The struggle
against uncivil conflict abandoned.

The right to accomplish the right
to accomplish, abandoned. The first place
and subsequent places abandoned to thoughts
fading into brilliance
one last one final time.

The majority of consequences abandoned,
the requirements of fear and the demands
of loss, abandoned, or thought to have been.
The dark form in the dream of prospects
clinched in a cliché, abandoned
for waking in a cold room, with forgotten moments
of loss, persistent still, and nothing obviously
missing, abandoned. Lack of sleep
finally abandoned in the recognition of insomnia.
The yard below, filled with abandoned car wrecks,
abandoned. The dread of Saturday, renewed
and impossible to abandon.

The bitter taste of vomit abandoned
to cold porcelain with tears and mucus
sliding into the drain.

Direction abandoned for journeys without
destination.
Destination abandoned at the moment
of recognition. The birthday celebration, abandoned.
The lost afternoon forsaken for the streets
between us, followed by potential but invisible
assailants, projecting their violence, abandoned.
The ruined house crippled by neglect,
abandoned by a previous occupant. We crush
a path of weeds to and from the door
in order to abandon it in turn.
The concert and the party in honour of

someone I do not know, abandoned.
The view of a face, a stranger, abandoned.
The view from the steps, and from the hillside
vantage point, and from the road around the peninsula,
abandoned. The gallery abandoned to a quiet
that inhabits the area despite our presence.
Was I ever there, abandoned?
A costly alternative and a cheap option
abandoned for no further action.

No further action abandoned.
The leak in the lean-to roof, abandoned.
The cracks in the ceiling that spread while
you are away, and I'm not looking, defying
the plasticity of vinyl paint, abandoned.

The impression of too many late nights,
abandoned for too many late nights. The difficulty
of getting back at such an hour, abandoned.
The proportion of the next page,
abandoned. The problem of curious regrets,
and their history, abandoned.
Further contact with arbitrary time limits abandoned,
having to cease from effons to locate,
and having made a connection, swiftly
to abandon it. This knowledge abandoned.

The green and fading park, and the grey sky
becoming blue again, abandoned. The wind
late at night, striking the leaves that abandon
their stems, as the season abandons, and is abandoned
in turn. The people I abandoned, who I need but
cannot approach. The fake reaction abandoned.
The airport abandoned, departing and returning.
The station and the bus-stop, abandoned by request only.

The problem of emphasis and styles of being,
nudging towards the perilous assumption, abandoned.

The restricting and the mundane, abandoned for the merely
ordinary. The questions and their answers.
The questions and the answers instantly abandoned.
The shards of a broken cup, scanered across the floor,
abandoned in a gathering dust. Unpleasant image.
The diminished and alarming alibi,
no longer appropriate, abandoned.

So this is how the pace changes.
Washing socks after walking all day
in search of entertainment, and what was escaped from.
Clumsy and sweating, like an awkward phrase.
It cannot be explained, it does not apply,
there is no further use for that particular
reactionary accusation. The water is tepid
and avoids the requirement of thirst.
The despair of the morning rises before me,
I give in and carry on.
Sunlight melts the frost. My new second-hand coat
resisting the cold wind.
Simple facts as a by-product of events
of insufficient intensity, that is the heart
of the matter. Hints, suggestions, redundant devices.
The contents of imagination abandoned.

This flexibility of random days we acquire
by default. Where are you, you ask I ask,
speaking through wires and clattering exchanges.
All the lives in all the buildings lit by theories
and propositions.
If I speak am I real?
If you answer are you there?

If you speak will I hear?
If you listen will I see?

It is time to continue and question accordingly.
Time to repair the force of circumstance. Time
to imitate the preparations of migrants
busily dismantling an evolutionary shift.
Time to catch the last train back before the take-
away closes, the lights go out, and the night stuns
us with sleep. Time to catch the train
of thought, so unbearable
and demanding, so unpredictable
and serious.

We left the house at first light. The light that
precedes dawn. Recent events curiously
transpired into one of those mystifying contortions
of the expected, abandoned like a sign of the times.

The neat phrase abandoned.
False information, presented in good faith, abandoned.
The truth, enough of that, abandoned.
Redressing the balance, abandoned.
Clothing, that precarious and diverse apparatus,
abandoned. The conversation you overhear,
eavesdropping at the edge of a precipice.
One step wrong that could be the foot in the door
of that sinking feeling.

The sense that changes to sensation,
and the tense to tension.
The problem is knowing what the problem is.

The probable breach, the ensuing rage,
the oblique ownership of credit,

this golden sunlight that could by mythical
if ill-used, taken as easy option,
abandoned.
Late rays carousing in the corners.
All we ever said, are saying now, and will say,
to the pure invention of tomorrow.
Nothing better than having the odds stacked
against you. This way you feel
the pressure, sense the reverberations of risk.
If you change your parting, have you changed
your mind? If you change your mind,
why wear your hair that way? Why
confuse the circumstances with vagueness?
This feeling, like walking
without a safety rail,
several storeys above street level.
Wearing shiny leather shoes to increase
the paranoia.
Attention to detail at the moment the telephone rings,
a cigarette drops into a cup of tea,
and the incident is recorded, and abandoned.

Another call from the unexpected.
It is darker earlier now it is autumn.
It is colder in the bus shelter where I wait
for a connection.
I am not ready but it will not stop.

Impossible to say enough about such pedestrian matters.
The curious conditions appropriate to natural disasters.
The uses to which we put the obvious dereliction
of historic remains, abandoned.
Symbolic trickery of the times. The contrite
and self-fulfilling prophecies of the past.
The matter of 'good taste' we allude to

by rising each morning, crumpled from a restless sleep,
hopping around on cold linoleum, filling the kettle
and searching for something sweet.
Why not stay in bed and discuss the spectacle of damp fog
swaying outside the window.
Leisure without guilt until three, when the afternoon
has all its bright and grandiose details
fading elaborately,
and it is too late for most intentions
to be accomplished, except for the one that allows
such plans to be abandoned,
as if the action, the potential, and the day,
stop right here.

Heroic and Hatless

The sun appeared, hinting and heroic,
a declaration of intent in the knowledge
of its place, here.

In a mangled thicket
the true enthusiast collects useful information
for an earnest commentary.

States of freedom.
Looking to replace the need
for looking.

The question to be put to you is only moments
away. These are not problems,
they are parts
of a life.

Awesome space, like a favourite dread,
dedicated to encroachment.
The shadow of being here, out of context,
out of hand, to celebrate.

The Berliner Allee is quiet
for a Friday night. On the corner,
in the Argentinian restaurant, no
one speaks English. I order
and eat in sign language with occasional words
and silence.
A German gaucho serves beer.

It is late and raining when I walk back
to my hotel.
The season dedicates its encroachment
to all those without a hat.

Right to Reply

You said nothing
moves like the body's
fluids move in time
with the heart.

You said
an approving glance
can be like a glancing blow
of native air
to the head.

Nothing moves.
Though the narrative moves
along regardless.
Fading into action.
Fading into action from your point
of view.

Plain daylight hours
of obligatory stillness.
Nothing moves
more arbitrarily
than movement.
The alternative,
the duplicity,
selection, stratagem.
Nothing, you said, moves.

Bypassing a direct source,
like the day passing,
like the day passing clear and empty.

Then recite, you said,
in the hours given.
The days are preset.
The format cross-referenced to fade.
Light running into shade.

No, nothing moves, he said.
Quote who?
Renaissance format of native air.
The day fades clear and empty.

Alias

This is a fiction.
This is a fiction and it answers back.
It answers by appointment, answers an obligation.
It answers on demand,
answers in some confusion, but
it answers.

The jacket will belong to the original owner
long after he has abandoned it.
The economics of need.

Factions form part of a general intent.

There is nothing to equal
a demonstrative gesture,
freely expressed, or a cold meat sandwich
in the cafe at the corner.

A cold meeting of hands and emotions
in the cafe at the corner.

During the evenings, with nowhere to go,
they would be there, caressing mutual abuse.

It is convenient to let the wind scatter
my father's ashes
through the grass, and a puzzle to decide
where to place future bouquets.

Higher education was the school up the road.

Snow brightens glooming winter days,
like an escape clause,
with its brilliance.
The forms of the familiar
are modified and disguised.
We dress and go out,
wearing our falsehoods.

There is nothing virtuous in virtue.
We are the signs of the time.
A hostile verification puts the cantankerous
proposition out of reach.
The cautionary tales suit all types of excess.

This is experience. Now and then.
Removed to safer keeping. The rumour
of past infringements
has nowhere to go.

Paying lip-service to a sneer.
Embraced at arms length.

"Do you remember Richard? He telephoned
for help. When they arrived they had to break
down the door. He was lying on his bed,
but they were too late to save him."
It is not the way you enter
it is how you choose to leave
that matters.

A searchlight probes the sky.
I invite you oblivious of your mission.
This is the past speaking. You know where
you are. A metaphysical language,
a direct approach, a charming proposal,
a dumb metaphor.
Let's date.

There is safety in numbers.
There is safety in numbers.
There is safety in numbers, so start counting.

Viewpoint

Gravity holds the lightest tread,
as though air was glue, and each step
a collision of ideologies,
and you do not want to toe the line.

You lose count of the number of steps
to the door. This is the hour.
It is already late when you enter,
a name gripped between your teeth.

You are arriving in another country
and the distance is equal to any other.
I wake here in your sleep, hear what you say,
and it might be so.

The precise recounting of the occasions
you were leaving for the last time.
The charm of irreconcilable differences,
the perfect timing of separate ways.

N.B.

You are alone,
but there is always the idea,
memory says so.
Clouds curl on the sky.
Were you previously
a star performer?
My column inches are
running out.
My word! what truth.
what fearless confrontation.
What? Truth?
Are you alone?
Let's talk about this
necessary exactness.
The silk of your passing
to where I am not.
Tell me your dream,
it is a just punishment.
There is a tear in
comfort's canopy.
The choice is yours.
Where is the chorus?
Where are the declarations
to protect against largesse?

Shadow Boxing

A nudge of air pauses over clammy lawns.
This is the height of the season.
Bright afternoon, lodged in your head,
shaken by sneezes.

That marvellous view is indisposed.
That shrubbery of colours, that grass
of ochre straw. That hand-bell clanging
through the evening veil, last visitors
departing through the closing gates,

the vague and twilit day rests assured.

A silent wind fans the suburbs where voices
murmur of the ache from dry heat,
stiff limbs, outlandish moods.

They diagnose mysterious ailments and
subversive ills, they mumble the stubborn
litany of their politics, that holds them
like a safety pin about to give,
a silhouette consumed by light.

And when you thought me cornered,
I threw a curve across the straight line
of your demonstration of the art
of shadow boxing.

A Perfect Language

Jets cruise in blank air
Still as ice.
Drawing thin white
Fading white broken
White lines
On clear brilliant twilight.
The perfect written language.
The perfect language
Of alien territory,
Dramatic and immense.
The eerie presence of a cry
In that perfect language.
A human cry in blank air.
In the fading language of the day,
The immense stillness of the sky,
The thin disintegrating broken lines.
The perfect alien language of the cry.
The perfect, the alien cry.

Four Songs

1

A car burns on the hard shoulder.
It is the unexpected taking a position.
The passengers watch the smoke blemish
drifting away; drifting back
to where some birds rise and fall,
flap and twist, awkwardly.
The verges shrug imperceptibly.
The outwardly perplexing eschews artifice.
Fine rain rains down on their shoulders.
Nothing stops, everything keeps moving,
moving towards this place, moving away.
Twisting lights of blue and orange
streak the air. This moment, this momentum,
the colours we see, the interference
of space moving away.

2

She said I don't suppose you believe,
we sat down, the firelight rippled
across the furniture, the photographs,
the heavy fabric across the window
and the door, the devil.
One morning I saw a rat walking across
the hall as I went towards the kitchen.
I watched it and it took no notice
of me at all, just kept on walking,
through the door into the kitchen,
and when I got there it had disappeared.
I called Tom and told him and he said,
Yes. I moved out that day, but it's taken
eleven years to reach here, alone.
I come and go. I read about the violence
in the newspapers. And now they've changed
the rooms around and I can't tell
which is which. I won't be going back
again.

3

Inside the house we wait for ever.
We wait for ever in extreme states
of mystery and passion, in the shadows
of subtle tedium.
At sunset the coarse horizon strikes
a careless but strategic line
between light and land. We are what
this light surrounds, absorbed by
eroding swathes of darkness,
like an anecdote retold to pass the time.
We are waiting, it is clear, for special
arrangements, a code of action. We are
waiting, there are voices outside,
they pass by This is dangerous earth,
the house will lose control.
A molecular restructuring will create
the words the house has emitted
over the years, and they will circulate
and there will be no mistakes,
and the message will be edited, phrased
and delivered faultlessly. They will be
a composite of the thoughts of the
occupants present past and future.
"Inside the house we wait for ever . . ."

4

There is no way of knowing. Now
I speculate. This is the place
for an unusual alliance. Transmission points
are calculated and identified.
Withstanding the pressures from immense
natural forces and unknown interferences
is sufficient proof.
The intention was other than what has become.
Innocence, devotion, making for the railway station.
The rippling lake surface fragments the moon's reflected
light. Deer grunt on the moor.
The forgotten number,
you know, the one you requested, listen.
River in flood.
The river into which a friend's father fell
and drowned, probably drunk because his business
was failing, and maybe, they said, it was no accident.
The river running along the valley
across which the signals flashed.
I turn, when I turn, I am there,
missing the signal. Leaving it.
By day there is a silence between two points.
It is communication without light.
It is speaking into air, it is waving through twilight.
Waving aimlessly in the haze rising from the valley,
where the river flows lightly across sand and stone,
at its normal level, less than ankle deep.

Caption Block

There had to be a context, a route,
some gift wrapping, a scene or two
short on monopoly. Too awkward,
too secular. Too dubious.

This street fills with people and cars.
A speciality of glossy remains, permitted
their lingering dilemmas.

The day passes along, provisionally exact.
There is hardly time to compose an insult.
Locks drawn back
to comfortable repose. Time
has some interesting aspects. Its duration
for instance,

your presence, the plans translated into
foiled procedures, the leisure
of political expediencies.

You may recall your presence there,
inspired and envied by knowing
no limit, like a bad dream.
A system of invitations and rebuttals,
the texture of the breakfast
at the beginning of your day off.

It does not resemble living in a caravan,
or any other familiar aspect
of your lifestyle. There is no
conviction, without first having prepared
for drastic action, the kind
that becomes an endless example
to us all.

And to us all the last echo of its
wailing lament, the crisp reigning of
an imminent spiritual exposure.
When it's tough outside tend to the right
and get some religion.
The role is crystal clear, it's simple life,
but pays a handsome dividend in
conscience cushioning.

If the resultant space bears a caption block,
it will read according to your needs.
Subjective to the last, that distant
glittering refinery of ideas,
the embodiment of opinion,
of uncorrupted facts. And the estuary beyond
flashes signals with the sun. I urge you, task,
reveal yourself. He stands in silt,
modified by upbringing
into a version.

Programmed responses jam on a re-learning
mode. Today it was easy, but I don't expect
further conclusions, and I have someone to see
out there. Later it will be a work of sustained
effort and concentration, a labour required
by the spirit, whatever its taste.
Tradition wears a tight-lipped smile on
a mean mouth.

"I needed that holiday, but it went
without me" A demon timetable served only
to confuse the connections.

Where a hotel provides dubious comforts,
cost is abstract, until the money runs out,
and a dismissive air won't even get you
to the revolving door. My advice would be,
protect yourself against one way traffic
refuse to answer questions, think logically
and with enthusiasm of the future, then go out
and find one. Distract yourself by taking a
walk. The sea front. The bilious sky.
Tennis in a sheltered court around the back.
If it is not your game allow the repetitive
"thwack" of the ball to lull you into sleep.

At breakfast the sea view accords some
nourishment to his flagging spirit.
It waved too high, and for too long.
Proud possessor of an attractive narrative,
let it go. Your desires are preposterous,
pitiful and ultimately pedestrian. You wanted
to be a painter and now you are not.

Something warned him not to turn around,
he did, but they had gone. Stubborn
extravagance. Try anything once. Try
shorter sentences for their music, and
their charm. Try nothing more to say.

The water was cold and cloudy. The sky
was cloudy and wet. The family divided.
A day later the sun shone. The status
of the fugitive, with surrounding fiction, is
questionable, but politically desirable

Stubborn extravagance preferred to 'good' advice.
There is another version that seeks
to present itself.
"That's no laughing matter"; we joked and smiled
about its curious structure, the mechanism
of muscular interaction, tensions and reflexes.

We grow a little older each time
'New Art' hits the fan.
I have a question for you,
in the future, beyond reasonable doubt.
In the attic he existed on a diet
of noodles and soup,
washing the dishes in the bath.

Your destination then, is now, is a belief
in progress principles via disruption,
a foray through the margins of
an 'underworld', and out,
like a gesture incapable of being
misinterpreted. But in England,
in the rural provinces, what hope
of leading anything but an aimless
entirely safe and convivial existence.

A surfeit of ill health, death, drastic
measures, conservative association and church
jumble sales, amateur dramatic society
farces. Activate the humour valves.
Turn the tap of the tea urn. An anthropology
of rural sentiment.

An object, falling through space,
meets an object falling through space.
They greet as fellow travellers
in the dip and swell of past infringements.

Every form employed. The spread, like
paint, applied in masterful strokes.
When, finally, he discovered he had
the knowledge that he was not a painter,
he relaxed.
It took time but, but he probably
clarified a point or two in the intermission;
intermission signing off.

In the Favourite Cafe for breakfast,
long before the owner is shot in a family feud.
The mellow drama of chipped formica and
processed peas. Saturday afternoons and
second-hand bargains.

One version was overpowering with threat.
I never rose to that occasion. A list
of names as token knowledge of the
event, but that was all.
No use in labouring to create dissatisfaction.
To do away with numbers, colour references,
and doltish imitations of false witness.

Preposterous desires in an attractive narrative.
Proud possessor of such a faculty.
No nonsense activists and wishful thinkers.
"You think I should return," he said.
This was a version. I know its dimensions.
They lived by a river.

The meadows's dispersal of golden yellow
marigolds; the car wrecks across the ditch,
stacked three high, blood stained interiors
decomposing in weather changes.

Cross country runners
struggle up the muddied slope, following
the trail of coloured paper strands.
Weekend exercise in landscapes of loss,
beneath shabby skies, defying the
bickering wind.
Rare migrant birds land provocatively
in the next field.
Mentioned brightness, speaking of colours.

They kicked in the door, ran crouching
against a rubble wall, armalites
tucked under armpits.
We passed the check point, on other business,
observing scenes from daily life.

"We lost our windows three times,
but the target is the housing department
across the street."
"A man I know has lost a leg, and his
doctor warns, the other is in danger, if he
continues to smoke. We drink in the same bar."
Two patrol vehicles, monstrous with mesh guards,
rumble across a waste ground of flattened
houses. Speaking of colours we wait for
silence. The insignia of intent.
The small change of serious comment. The question
of what you wear on your sleeve.

The condition of the city.
Education, commerce, social exchanges,
law and order violence, terrorist violence.
A death threat loiters with intent. A concealed weapon.
But you are from somewhere else and plan
to leave, remember? And the hill and
the mist and the housing schemes and
the real sense of foreboding and pain
along the two Roads; and the one bright
warm sunny day when it was necessary
to report an appalling sense of unease
drifting in the streets.

Droll correspondent, this is a case for a revival.
Wit rescue, come to our aid. Amusing twist,
turn your hand to smart comment.
All the protagonists threaten you with their
ultimate weapon, your own conditioning.

Feeling what, at the sound of laughter?
Check it. Progress report by way of under
cover agencies. Consider yourself to be convinced.
But by whose smile, aspirations, obsessions,
displacement, commemorative celebration?

Rural Pursuits

    1

The journey out
and the return.
Any moment
is what I am waiting for.
A curious regression
in time takes hold.
Simply registered,
unbearable beyond words.
Beyond words
where the persistent sense
is one of waiting,
of an interlude
hindered at last by impatience.
Where no return is mistaken
for arriving, and arriving
is only an interlude in something
of much grander scale,
that may fail exactly
as words fail to materialise
in appropriate manner.
This assumption is another strategy
composed of dissimilar events.
And so disorder preconceived
is heir to deceit.
No artifacts, remains, or tangible
evidence to produce.
History in the making.
An immaculate shift.
A shift reflected on opaque windows,
where this future will materialise
from that past,

and we breathe again, suddenly,
relieved of counter-claims,
assumptions and returns.

2

This road. I know this road.
This road I know. This road.
Have we spoken of familiarity?
It seems familiar, it may be
a theory, could it be
an accomplishment?
Before the journey
there is a road.
There was a road. I visited long ago,
I did not return.
Some people call
this place their home.
I know these fields, these trees,
those buildings.
Some people live here, I come here
with a journey in mind.
This journey.
I know this journey.
This journey is familiar.
I have not been here before.
Can you tell me the way
to the next town?
Can you?

I know this road. This road
to the next town. Have I ever been here
before?
Look, that group of buildings, that hill,
this junction.
This sensation. I know this sensation.
It is being here, it is recognition,
it belongs with travelling
this road.

I know this place.
I have never been here before.
Today is the first time.
Do I know this road? Can you tell me,
can you, do you know this road?

3

At this hour the silence.
In the suburbs an uneasy cry, Business as usual.

An owl swoops between aerials, chimneys
and shadows. Business as usual.
Fear paces a room. Business as usual.
Familiar artifacts furnish the emptiness.

If you listen, it is the commonplace
shifting around, that prevents sleep.
Silence colliding softly
with its echo.
The shapely ears on a tilted head,
listening in to the relentless waves
of sounds.

Mist on the hill is hooked
to its surface by dwarf oaks.
rock outcrops and coarse grasses.
The house with the white gate,
with the shrubbery and the stream
at the end of the sloping lawn,
settles for the evening
in a pink and lurid glow.

It is so far away, the clicking
of locks and window catches
can not be heard.
It is so far away, the voices,
what they say, how they sound,
and when they speak, and when they are silent,
and when they speak again,
can not be heard.

At this hour, where you have gone
comes to the same place,
and something that did not happen once,
long ago, does not happen now, here.

When you arrive, they have moved on,
any moment now,
to where you are.

4

He was driving and it was dark.
He was driving in the darkness of winter,
towards the house. Lights were visible
over the hedges, beyond the fields,
in the distance, in the darkness,
in the winter darkness.
The sky was blue-black, flickering
with starlight. He was driving and
it was dark, and for a moment, for one shadowy
moment, illuminated by dial-light,
it was another time, another occasion,
travelling the same road.
It was another time on this same road.
A hand reached into the car, reached in
from the darkness, from the winter darkness,
reached into his body, reached through
flesh, muscle, blood and tissue.
A savage hand that gripped the organs
resting there, that gripped and released and
pulled away. That bruised, released
and drew back, retreating into a deeper shadow
swiftly passing. A shadow of nausea,
a concentration of pain and darkness.
A winter darkness through which he was driving,
towards the lights. The lights at the base-line
of the sky. Towards the lights, coldly,
steadily, glowing.
Towards the cold glowing lights
in the darkness.

Stepping Out

The lines of communication
Are down.
The line of least
Resistance is difficult
To follow.
The lines we read
Between are crossed and double-crossed.
Having a means to
An end is meaningless
And endless

The quandary for the questioner
Is no face
To answer to.
He is a figment
Of his imagination,
The best friend
He never had.

The day here is warm
For the time of year.
It transmits a proposal.
We speak
Only to accommodate
Exterior accomplishments.
You are made available
To inspiration.

Sense of direction,
Generally reliable, fails to link
Essential co-ordinates.
Departing, they rise
To the occasion.

Dress is optional.
The assault of tedium
Is thwarted.

Ambushed in bathroom steam,
Touching the hand
That wipes the mirror
From the other side.

Distracted from a precise and
Conscious management of memories.
He arrives on his way there.
Passing through
A state of suspicion and martial law.

Freedom is
A condition of the mind,
He thought he thought.

You wake, you sleep,
You wake again.
The disturbing composition of
Another day.
The missing element.
The north point of your present need.

The type of phrase
You never use.
A curious calumny
And scent of truth.
Further demonstrations
Of contemporary talent.

Work and anxiety
Go hand in hand,

Or hand in glove,
And up to no good.
The odds
Are definitely odd.

The tide is out.
Sunlight ripples passionately
On river mud,
In August.
For a moment,
In August in the kitchen,
In sunlight through
The door.
Basic image, witty rejoinder,
Natural disaster.
We own
These words.

Barrels rest across steady arms.
Fingers pull back
The shades from frightening
Heroism in minds
Dulled by order.

This is like sleep,
It obliterates light
In another country,
And it hurts.

Some of what I like
About today
Is some of what I have
forgotten.

So unexpected, so arcane.
They are playing
Our song,

And the voice is
The voice
Of overall control.

Cold and calmly rejoicing.
The lack-
Lustre charm
Of the "right" word.
The eyes of those caring
To notice.
Inconsolable and isolate.
The treatment promotes
Health in all who entertain
Uncertainty. Nothing so
Clear as the right directions
In the wrong town.

You side-step to avoid
Innuendo.
Is this a turning point?
Are those the bright heels
Of memory, relinquished.
Guessing their way
Into the narrator's purpose.
Stepping out?

Mutant Generation

Air moves wet and westerly.
So, spring.
So, space.
So, mutant generation.
Matrix manifestation.
Cut to overview. Cut to blue
sky.
Cut to back
ground translucent intersection.
Confirm and acknowledge.
I dream of never sleeping.
The sky goes blank, starless.
So, nothing but.
So, wind wet and westerly,
and wide awake.
So, dream of spring,
of space, of never sleeping.
Never sleeping.
Of spring air space
the taste of salt from lip
to tongue.
It is a delirious confrontation,
a certain festival of what
we hope to find.

Song 5 (out of sequence)

Daybreak's after-image in the light,
the unearthly light of generous summer.
Leave the door open.
The future rests briefly in pre-alarm stillness,
without sound, without movement,
without benefit of hindsight.
The wreckage of jargon fragments.
The wisdom of inert specimens.
Walking among ruins in the dawn.
Disintegration on a blank screen.
Each image capitulating.
Jet me to an adjacent place
where I might meet the unrecognisable.
A raiding party gathered in readiness.
This is the future.
The door is open, and then
we move, and the light moves,
and the sound of its moving
in the stillness is the sound of voices
after they have spoken.
Is the silence of the voices ceasing.
The stillness after speech,
after movement. The end
and the beginning in their fabulous
trickery of finite proclamations.
This is the slow movement,
and this the crescendo.

Song 6

Streamers across the face of the moon.
The pull of strategic forces.
Here comes a moment . . .
What is that?

Vapour trails across morning blue.
By the light of the silvery . . .
No one remains.

The anthem for malcontents continues,
Off key and beside the point.

Here comes the bitter rain.
Here come the bright dancers.
Here comes a silvery calm.
Here comes the moment
You have been waiting for.

There goes the blunt instrument
Of your charm.
Here come March winds in April.
No one is looking.
No one remains.

A speaker addresses the dark auditorium.
This is what the moment we have been waiting for
will be like.
Here falls the bitter rain.
Here fall the bright dancers.
Here flickers a silvery light.

No one is looking.
No one is looking.
No one is looking because no
One remains.

For the Record
In memory of Donald Macrae

    1.

When you returned
to the side ward,
it was too late for tea.
I did all the talking.
You managed a smile, a nod,
and a glance at the window,
signalling hot blue summer day.

That investment in the present
left you exhausted.

I touched your hand, but could not
ask for a reply
to the moment's incapacity
to fulfil your need.

You slip away
into the light before me,
into the enthralling light,
into the light
breathing neat air
through a mask of diminishing returns.

2.

Your hand held high and open
as I leave, to walk through white corridors
ruffled with June heat.

The thought that you will die,
impatient with the final exchanges,
written by a trembling arm
grown thin,
plotting future delineations
of events beyond you.

In a photograph, the likeness
is no longer real
but an image dimensionally suspect.
It is you, but you are no longer within
that territorial embrace.

This unplanned, untimely
and impertinent wasting,
impossible to check or foil,
bearing down
to assuage the void.

LCD Ode

It will be a day like this day,
a day of many familiarities, many certainties,
a day never to be forgotten.
A day whose aftermath, never to be forgotten,
will arrive unannounced,
fittingly, composed in every detail.
And knowing, being a part, will in turn
become the principle desired,
as the time element hovers
in liquid crystal display.
Text memory, word search, phrase control.
Living in the screen,
humming a serial theme.
A day of glowing amber, glowing green.
Communications systems set to respond,
flickering under glass.
Exposed to intermittent light,
floating like a banner through air
impossible to possess,
explained in particles and shadows
on the kitchen floor,
the variations leave to drift
in consequent uniformity,
never to experience the quickening
result of touch.
No light and shade to raise issue
with the seasons' slip,
as evening casts autumn on to the leaves,
and the dreadful screen
deceives the operator's eye with lost remarks.
The message be a plea for scrutiny

before the final blank display
emits its certain empty light.
Like no dark could ever be,
unless devoid of you.

Par Avion

Waves blind the flat sand.
Each day's surface aspires to
the texture of change, the gloss
of sliding water matching the sky.
This is a story told in reverse.
All these tidy roads deserted.
The wind pursues its purpose
through towering foliage,
its push carries each crest
into the next, and back again.
The trees are clearly visible, from the door
the sky becomes a declaration
of mundane symbols. Its fault line
under stress, an articulation of metaphor.
I listen in the prevailing silence
which harbours the tough hum
of general activity. I listen, not to words,
but to the voice,
the sound of the voice speaking.
The pattern in the words.
The wind as it passes, as time passes,
as the lights are extinguished
by the separation of the power source
from endless shining.
Words at the confluence of stillness
and controlled presentation.
The sand has moved.
The sound has absorbed the silence
in exchanges of resonance and modulation.
The table stands between my sleeve
and something blue.
The hollowness of the hour
is a dumb witness to the narrative.

Light and space separate. The preferred
configuration arises from this singularity
as a word, whose music invokes intricate nuances,
is forgotten before it can be transcribed,
its memory of itself lasting beyond
the probable limit of desire.

As It Is

A faint haze of smoke,
coloured amber by the afternoon
sunlight, spreads across
the city. Its definition
is vague, its origin, pollution.
I think you are in the vicinity
when you are far away.
Imagination places your presence
like a thought crossing my mind,
as I cross the street
after rain.
The silence of intuition
mingles with the muted roar
of jets, homing in
to the broad flat diagram
of concrete runways.
The beyond of darkness falling,
edged with lemon light,
with phosphorescence,
with a flaring aura of light relief.
The beyond that embraces emptiness,
that you have named
as your gift.
It seemed for a moment
the way was lost.
It seemed for a moment your presence
crossed into future wishes,
but it is merely the intuition
of silence, hovering with reflections
cast by glass walls.
The reflections of an opposite
far away.

Varations on Silence and Figures in a Room
For John Davies

When we speak
we hear
silence, silence
rumbling from afar.

Space is a word,
a word in a room
in which we stand,
various and diverse.

A failed alliance.
A lost continent
of the imagination.

Parallel forces.
Serene restraint.

Silence, silence
tumbling from afar.

An unobtainable tone.
A redundant number.
Fabricated exchange.

Exhibition dance steps.
Magenta light.
Silent light.
Silent magenta light.

Provocative reflex
(Stay still).
Outstretched limbs
(Say so).

Unobtainable tone
(Try again).
Secondary process
(Primary urge).

Silent light.
Magenta light.
Silent magenta light.

Try again.
Silence.
Try again.
Silence, silence
tumbling
from afar.

Tone of disconnection.
Tone of irony.
Continuous tone
of sultry light.

Fixed, expressionless.
Overwhelming and remote,
accomplished in
its implacable grace.

When we are silent
we hear words,
we hear words
tumbling,
words tumbling
from afar.

Silence and words.

Silence and words
from afar.

Ferrying

The co-ordinates of emotional dismissal
intersect predictably in the lyrics
of popular songs.

You were not mistaken.
It is fundamental to the process
of territories about to be redefined,
that the response is,
confront and protect.

The salvage of abandoned language
occupies a place between
trepidation and clumsy remarks.

A mind at work
is incidental
in an afternoon at rest.
Light falls across the ornate facade
on the other side of the street.
I saw you walking by
through the rucks and creases
of its trembling.

The same now as before.
This time.
Here in advance of our need.

White spray dances on the wind's lip.
Waves fall back to grey swell
surging.

As we pass between the islands.
the bow dips and rises
through the current's converging tussle.

I saw you there.
I wrote the words
lest they be forgotten.
You were not mistaken.
You were absent,
here in advance of the relentless ebb,
the incessant flow,
of the dark tides wandering.

Warnings

Here is the discontent
and here the angst.
This is a private function
and this the adornment.
Here is a message and there is the reply.
Here is a message.
There is no reply.

Here is a fumbling embrace,
and there are the cool stars,
there are the cool, aching stars.
You are the witness, the participant;
you are the willing observer, the protagonist.
Here is the platform
and the acknowledgement of hands.

There is the control.
here is the switch.
There is the warning light
and here is the warning.
The control, the switch,
the light, the warning.
Here comes the patrol.

This is the information,
the litany of voices and static.
This is the main square,
there is the dry fountain.
Portable barricades are stacked
along the pavement
There are the empty streets.
Here are the empty streets,
It is cold.
The cold of starlight.
A stellar cold, the chill of separation.

You walk through the barriers.
You carry a message
in a dormant section of your mind.
Walls crackle with the accumulation
of knowledge.
Here is a place tuned to an aftermath.
There are the marks of progress,
love and desperation.

It is a fine late winter evening, daylight
reluctantly obliterated. Iridescent windows
fade to a formal grid of artificial light.
Somewhere someone lifts their head,
stands and walks out, walks out
into fragile pungent air.

Tongues of Light

Of the available conversations,
the electric, the enchanted song,
the telegraphic traced on to airwaves,
these provide only part
of the communication procedure.
Vision slides to a blur.
Hearing pleads.

Discovering the recorded message,
attempts to breach its structure
are foiled by the continuous loop
of repetition.
The cominuous loop of repetition.

All is perpetual motion.
Facts retell even that which has been
systematically obliterated.
The windows are open
but the door is locked.
There is a fine edge,
a high altitude twilight,
a vast expanse of persistent reasoning.

There is the advance of civilisation
and the retreat from metaphor.
We speak a migrant tongue.
We surpass understanding.
We deny the enchantment of pain.

A delicate embrace of live terminals.
The exchange of visual contact.
Touch,
etched on sensitive air,
between transmission points.

Tongues of disturbed current.
Tongues of light.
Tongues of dark fire.
The immaculate collaboration of tongues
of light.

The Edge (1993)

Foreword

In memory's wilderness
Alphabet of beast tracks
Marks the empty road
Neutral curiosity invents
Questions of procedure
Tentative footsteps traverse
Remote Asiatic plains
The caravans of spice merchants
Welcome us expecting trade
Offering hospitality
Plumes of delirious dust impregnate
The material woven in cunning dreams
Fertile pastures relinquished to fallow
Land economics confound
The transient labour force
Whose trade is erased
Farms surrendered to ruin
Signify audacious outposts of failure
Erosion wounds exposed through ground cover
Reveal millstone grit
And glacial junk united
Beneath a tangled shawl of barren excess
Low cloud delivers fine rain
Anointing Three Shires Head
Upper Swineseye, Red Brook, Spittal House
The six terraced cottages of Varden Town
Elms and pylons stoutly attending
The vacant quarters
Where fields obtrude at Fitton Town
In the garden of the local coal merchant
And preacher
A rampant lilac spreads
Like an unedited anecdote
From fear that disruption might weaken
The earth's crust

To expose a yawning pit
Damnation's door, Hell's lobby
The demon profile of studded leather cowl
Transferred ranting to the pulpit
The Dipping Stone, Yearns Low, Cold Arbour
Orpheus from the underworld
Duane Eddy in the yellow light of late summer
Where fields reaped clean
Surrender their fecundity
Desires lie mutilated
Running dark and wanton
In extremis

✻

Motive connects proposition
To exploration
And by such a manoeuvre
Gains an angst laden response
Debt prospers where air strikes
Thin lines of chance
Across his face
A membrane of white ice
Suspended between furrows
Set by a practised eye
Enhances the silence of perspective
Honest curiosity and familiar solitude
Fabricate a devious pattern
Belligerently overt in mellow brilliance
Plough blades cast an alien mark
Into the land's inclined platform
Empty hands intrude
Demanding a page
Withdrawing a word
Shaping the sense of enquiry
Imagination grafts a cast of shadows
From impenetrable confusion
Where desire pleads terrible enchantment
And severed patterns emerge
In the diminishing wake of strict attention

✹

Comparisons and similarities
Change everything
Events compare alternating forces
Words of inadequate conviction
Settle to brooding eloquence
Coordinates attach to the extremes
Of invisible communication
And indivisible conjugation
Walking through green and empty sunlight
From clearing to thicket
I stumbled once confused on two bodies embracing
Love and death in the ferns
Averting my inquisitive gaze of recognition
I lay in the damp pressure of ecstasy
The wordless conflict of penetration
Choked by weeds
Crawled then to the luminous end
Of the day
Where you go oblivious ahead of me

❉

Constant terrestrial adoration
Turning stubble blind
Procession of particulars
Begin again he speaks he is gone
Dispatched to search
You follow the arc of the shrubbery
To the kitchen door
Name a purpose and retreat
Not wanted there to censor talk
And tea sipping
Follow the curved driveway
Like a glistening claw
Across the lawn
Gouging root's white filigree
From dark to buoyant air
Labouring against harm
Which is given by the unflinching grip
Of feudal control

❈

Trodden earth resists the heel of penury
Stamping its need dedicating the track
November mist rising to haunt
Labour's sparse precinct
To fade in shifty airborne celebration
Distressed though pliant always to demand
Damned English landscape progenitor
Of herbaceous livery dulled
By a gauze of darkness lying folded there
You watch you are silent you wait
Headlights sweep the mottled wall
You wait grow cold amidst the details
Of tribal inheritance
The magnetic sky sparks and flickers
Running through fever drench delirium
Eyelids stretched across double vision
The retina resists with a blink
You watch you are silent you wait
Headlights sweep the empty wall
You wait you are silent
You watch you are silent
You wait

✺

Tell me no name bequeath no toil
Mark no informal contract
Observe no obligation
No pagan inspiration
Proud independence demands
Your servile response
Quit raw circumstance define action
Birds arrive to scavenge
At the furrow's overlay
Replete with vulnerable energy
And fragile system's obedient repose
Dust coyly espousing weak bindings
Of sour light
Cool and subtle change
As the edge of sleep sidles
Like a stain from the melting fields
As you welcome and softly breath
A drift of lazy limitless air
Into the chamber of the night

❋

Subliminal desires exploit
The dictatorship of the word
Though circumstance controls
The space they inhabit
While you waited impatiently
For a weather report to plot
Your day I watched a running cloud
Torn and reshaped repeatedly
Across the restless adornment
Of challenging overcast
The word applies when need
Displays its turbulent presence
And a remedy encompasses the flaw
Meeting vacant possession
With unreasonable demands
Humility grunts where objections
Fester and the days of labour
Decrease in effectiveness and number

※

Art probe annuls waste
Material desires subvert chance encounters
This bleak reductive conformity
Moves amongst perennial outbursts
In the future recorded voices will commence
Like engines fired simultaneously
Impression and interpretation ratified
Light broadcast into troubled folds
Whose mystery is one part allure
And nine parts misery
The numbering bestows authority
On blades that slice and separate
The stable crop outgrown by need

✽

At the time of your departure
You exchange the burden of silent judgment
For familiar absence
Mount the old black Raleigh
And pedal away
Spokes of glistening light fragmented
By black boots turning
Coat tied with string
Grey trilby
Stained around the band
Intense morning light tilted over
Your passing form head and shoulders
Above the laid hawthorn
A silhouette of eager geometry transformed
By the brilliant wash of late September sun
Negotiations remained unresolved
In homage to the retreat from false calm
In this act of departure
All movement is stunned by silence
That bears the rebuke of laden stares
Guilt festers at the heart
Quilted cloud barricades the blue
All manner of natural and artificial
Representations clamour to be heard
Wings beat arms encircle absence
And rage clots to mucus on bloodless lips
A terrible constriction a contamination
Of dialogue set free into a songless terrain
Lip reading the names of ancient sources
And future requirements
That they might materialise to claim their due
Chanting persistently against time's clamour

❋

Echoes vibrate through frowsy evening light
Transmitting a star map to this outpost
Of nocturnal exchange
The isolated range-finder lost for words
In an illuminated kiosk passed midnight
Press button A to speak
Or B to retrieve
The financial commitment to communication
Imagine being there
The dark swirling spiral of a voice rising
From an immense distance to connect
The light bulb burning a hole in darkness
Released to silence
Preparations of avoidance close down the sentence
Reawaken with the bragging sun
That putrid growth of singular conceit
Out and away before early moves
Harness thought
Provoked into defensive endurance

✺

Energy defined by the excess it harbours
Listen, listen to the door slam
Selected versions where restraint prevails
Waste of servitude and graceless allegiance

That Angels burn with deviant fervour
Whose thirst is quenched at a holy well
Water from blue rock to lips devouring
Listen, listen to the door slam

Reckless spasms of the tongue's swift accomplishment
Dreaming air against light and shadow on bruised flesh
Beyond words days of silence
Beyond silence the realm of the senses roused anew
The art of landscape its code of parallels

Listen, listen to the door, listen to the door slam
The day crumbling from darkness into view like
A version of itself with nothing to add

The Nation's backdrop the age of absent language
Fear to come no matter the otherwise intervention
Of future entitlement I dreamed your name
Falling through stars and blood
It was not spoken it fell
In the light, fell through and was the light
Lay across the surface of a lake returning its blank
But frenzied articulations
Listen, listen to the door, listen to
The door slam

Spoken at last into the silence of the last light
As it absorbs the effortless speculation
Residing there
Light denied as you listen, listen to the empty space

The example of absence from hearth and home
As if that light in flourishing would replenish
Absent colours an order of tones
A range of hues, a comfort of sound

Many are the routes and ways and many the times
To look back, remembering their sweet enticements
This other witness this curious revenge
They too are known to you, invading days
The eternal limitless presence of that light
Over that land, stagnant pools, responses, the lack

Grieve and be mortal, imagination exile and amusements
The language will rearrange the dispossessed
These days are not forever

Listen, these days, forever

❋

You were alone in your room
Writing a letter. Composing a message.
A message from the silence.
You heard the door open. Footsteps
Crossing the floor. Another door,
A door locked for many years, open
And close. The house was empty.
No one to disturb your task.
You were alone. Engrossed.
Writing a letter. It was as though
The room, expressing an obligation,
Had reconsidered something not resolved,
Searching for a way through falling air
Endlessly falling to stillness
Among the invisible shadows of absence
Between two states
Enlivened by the subversive nature
Of your veneration.
This is a ghost story in the old tradition.
The ghost is language and its spirit
of unrest. The haunting is the restless
spirit of words searching to communicate
You were claiming these words
Light and silence spinning a thread
and all the doors were flung open
to the future standing there
the tyranny of the future signalling
at the threshold the ghost of your future
working like a memory an illusion
spewing ectoplasm from the stillness
your future through the unborn
Entering and leaving the language of the room
the message like a latch dropping

into a keep and your companions were out
in the sun and you were alone there
and who passed by into the future
looking back through the emptiness
carried on then forward to subsequent meetings
answering the question
the question of recall unachieved
of missing evidence of proof unavailable
corroboration of the question asked
to remain there unfulfilled

❋

As much about not retelling
As wanting to know all universal truths

As much about the desire for expression
As meaning to expose

As much about exposure
As showing truth to be various

As much about demanding rights
As bearing the weight of futile guilt

As much about a legacy of independent comment
As the role of resolute messenger from the stars

As much about a face half turned towards a plea
As about mind games transmitters and perfect diction

As much about not now
As what then

As much about rural deprivation
As about monumentalism in the constructs of art

As much about nothing more
As so much to add

As much about a public outcry
As reports of false witness and anxiety's invention

As much about spirit technicians
As reality transferred in a bleached landscape

Where your footsteps are absorbed by tangled grasses
Over the blind kingdom of moles and worms

Awaiting the tribes to re-inhabit this dimension
Rising from clay and ashes

The ritual of nomadic celebration
The lost songs of imminent departure

❋

Random probes dispatched to aimless wandering
Explore the glorious space of influence
Determination and chance surface tensions
Shudder in the skin their blind response
Obedient to ambiguous directives
Diligent and attentive the dancers refuse
To wait balanced in a field of speculation
And passion moving through landscape's machinery
Whose tangency encounters your propinquity
Salute the implication of covert directives
That describes a pattern a confiscated diagram
Traced from the movements of your desire
In this the end
A gate a door a vanishing point
Recall the rising shift of sensuous light
The vanquishing drift propelled from a heartless desire
Blind words crawling to the distant page
Like scar tissue like the harvest and its product
Like the energy released when you close your eyes
The journey made precarious under an influence
Of latent passions
Linked to the stars
Incapable of forming your name

❋

Though dead and lost
Your minor prophecies claim attention
As among the riven fields I stumble
Across random sites that yield annually
To market forces and the feudal purse

Though long dead the loss sends out
Its memorandum as brief reminder
One day is blue and green and capable
The next a question of forgotten names
That reconnoitres for placement
In salvaged comparisons
Village without centre
The coming and going of the inhabitants
Why write of it when nothing else claims notice
When in wrongful opposition notorious truth
Claims that privilege

Forever demanding that a question
Infiltrates the soil where your footsteps
Print a direction you are familiar with
And from which you will turn
To dispute the answer

❋

Sometimes music too is inadequate
Has no power is incapable of excluding violation
The anniversary declines revelry
Measured time as stimulant register
Gone blank
Erotic sensors fallen like scales
From flayed limbs
Welcomed seed arranges its harvest
Settling pagan debt
With ritual homage
This window bleeding last late light
Across a body of words
Of symbols marking space
Between the hands and imagination
Dark cleft and tethered gesture
Buoyant state of verisimilitude
Conduit of improvised ideas
Shadows of unthinkable registration
Exhumed from a skull's open portals
Superimposed on another line of least resistance
A body rising from dark water
Shedding clear drops onto a body rising
The outstretched hand
And through the fingers
Atrophied in isolation

✻

Many ways and many other ways
Many variations on many ways
And many variations on many other ways
Some here and some now
Between this and between that possibility
What will become and what will be created
Gathering events of circuitous intention
A moment's predicted collision
Ways converge
Variations orchestrate intervention
Some remain benign while others generate
Spectacular response
Some are preternatural occurrences
Absorbed through layers of recall
Aspirations desires and dreams
Broadcast in the hiss and squeak
Of poor reception
We listen to the informing voice
Receive the signals and strains
In this redoubtable exchange of random patterns
Through September weld-light anchoring
Sometimes you open your eyes once more available
Or closing them defeat the legible presence
Of indefinite repose

❋

Wherever you settle contradicts
The evidence of a self-deluding quest
Take this chronicle this exploration
This act of recall
Addressing continuity
In previous examinations of forgetting
A linear constant insists
In spite of resistance
Self control ratifies the proposal
That liberates future procession
The temperature slips a degree or two
Without guide without pretence
Numbed by an alien regime
Modifications are unquestionably malign
Secondary after-image of your presence
Advances intact abdicating control
Direct current to present tense
Past reactions to the whole truth in time of peril
As summer night deletes another cumbersome day
And the chambered region of your mind takes heart
And comes to understand genetic influence
Mapped onto the subject's primary response
Thoughts pivot across the earth's curve
Systematically exposed to a revelation of words
That beset preconception and its implied understanding
Of benign contempt yoked to symptoms
And complexities of desire expressed
A flag of extreme celebration salutes
Such niggardly rebuke twitching through air's entanglements
Death's fix cavorts with fractured dialogue
Bleached raiment's hiss as you pass

As you turn a corner and the lush meadows
Deploy their hideous green laced with vetch
Host to an extreme celebration of flora
Glistening rush of boundless light
Where recurrent images laden with truth
Continually move away
Tracking the flawed course of unnatural lineage

❋

How you describe how it was then.
How it informs you. That time to which you refer.
Not one's own time. Walk with me. Share this
restless motion. How it was then.
To change places.
The land another's claim. A roof.
Not one's own roof. A room. Not one's own room.
Pay and hours conditional. Shelter and food adequate.
Dormant rage. Mark the passing. Freedom limited.
Narrative crop rotation. Land that belongs.
Not one's own land. Earth to earth. Walk with me.
The migrant homeless. How it was then.
Instruct the hours. Those years. Blocked to deter
infringement. Those times recalled that they might cease
to trouble you. Not one's own time. One bright morning.
Hollow light and iced channels. Snow fixed
along the eaves. Icicles thick as your fore-arm.
He said, we left our boots inside the door.
On the tiles inside the kitchen door. Ate breakfast
as the snow melted into muddy pools. He said,
she raged. The farmer's wife threw each boot into the yard.
We said nothing. He said, not one word of protest.
Walking into the snow to pair them. How it was.
Ascendancy of time's conflicts. To return that rage.
His own rage. Walk with me. Beyond the frame
of this retelling. How you describe how it was then.
Walk with me. Silent. No word.
Not forgotten, but given energy through the telling.
That you might close the door. Seal that vindictive eye.
Express the limits. Mark the passing.

Coda

The events and experiences that inform this work are interpretations of my father's anecdotal recall. After a short period in a cotton mill he worked as a farm labourer through the 1920s and 30s. After the second World War he transferred his efforts to gardening.

The underlying dissatisfaction and frustration with conditions that he accepted as unalterable, in an archaic and feudal system, remained with him into old age. He maintained that landowners and tenant farmers exercised choice preference for non-union men who would not cause trouble. This suited his migrant nature but certainly contributed to exploitation.

Illegitimate, and fostered at thirty days of age to a family of whom he rarely spoke; he carried that loss and its legacy throughout his working life, seeking to displace the influence in a glorification of family life that often confounded his best intentions.

This theme and exploration, both directly and through a form of observed, secondary presentation as witness, are jointly therefore about self-deception, conflict and continuity.

Art for Others (1998)

Art for Others

1

A daub's smudge catches a garment's hem
Clay ooze lips the boot's welt.
Fringe of scum.
Unkempt strands caught and dispersed
across broken spears.
Entering night's fragile gate.
Entering the access code of vile cries.
I have noticed flesh leak freely.
Malicious tyrant staking the open ground
pacing the veranda kicking the cinder path.
Hot fluid spurting into the empty lodging
relieved by an opposite force.
Windows similar to lights caught out
by opened clouds blossom but only in words
and fabrications allotted.
Allusions then. Probably dreams.
Probably not.
What is the meaning of a colour
with a name against it.
Unable to continue. The action of the gate.
At nightfall I am eating bread. The air
is impossible. Chill of disturbed sleep.
Days askew and uncounted.
A man with lips of mud. A kiss from within.
Sense and its surroundings. Not to be written.
Where progress might lead. Where it might
gather to itself as shadows to darkness.
Imagine. Having to endure a landscape.
It moves. It traces limits. It is boundless.
It proclaims its art for others to manipulate.
The rain falls in immeasurable fragments.

Could this be a spacious pavilion.
Emotions like warnings scatter before you.
This is my nation and with it my rejection.
I know nothing of country that does not decay,
augmenting the misery of its name.
Believe me who will not listen.
Avoid me as I seek revenge and retribution.
Console me in my absence, because of my absence,
console my absence in place of me.

2

Little to add, separately.
The blue noose against a cloudless sky
is almost inevitable.
The death it surrounds less than the shimmer
of heat haze distortion
swaying so slightly in the end-on presentation
the southerly seeks to achieve.
Then the dead hours single out the activity
most desired and you are forced to cancel.
Anger recouped from fear of retribution.
Froth and warped time bestow their favours.
By day you fabricate a future, there are lights,
a stage and many intense moments of adoration,
by night the decorative alliance sets its fix
and dances through the chemical eye.
Blessed are the curators of the many rooms
where books exchange their contents
and the earth heaves and twists
against offered limb or torso.
I had these ideas,
thought to escape their dreamy persuasion,
they follow in the slipstream of demented ideals
breaking like a comet bright and suddenly
annihilated in sunless space.
But whatever exercise I employ, whatever device
or regressive manipulation, the true displacement
eludes me, slides away, tide struck
on a wave of sinister forgetfulness.
Derelict day, invisible distance, their song.
Replace the receiver and continue to talk,
talk softly, calmly, with assurance.

My tongue slips across the words as they haunt
the faithless superstructure of your generous breath.
Continue to talk, communicate in the language
of phantoms, matter respects its given laws,
sound and light obey consequential demonstrations.
Self precludes authentic rehearsal of many changes.
Some of these began with something someone said.
Others endorse the supremacy of the human
whose development process illuminates the eye
as darkness at the back of the mind
issues an ultimatum though we continue
and our light with day makes fuse.

3

Here to collect warnings
rise like crows to a gun shot. The crowd salutes
a forgotten frontier.
Lay in darkness against a wall
waiting to outwit the supreme law
of management.
Came back for more.
Approached as though previously accosted.
Miraculous achievements and other alien compliments.
No good will.
Crave indulgence
but without contradictory excess.
I have time although not on my side,
it surrounds and to some extent anticipates
the exact moment.
Refuse to whistle the anthem
of the noise abatement society.
Junction of the soul.
During the excursion a necessary detour
slips in and out of his mind
like a perfect phrase at night without pen
or paper, it is fate and entirely plausible.
Examples provide themselves, magnanimously.
Source accumulations is a rare form
of pre-operative therapy, acute
and often elusive to the selected host.
Somewhat like the length of the road
taken in error, that exaggerates the time/
distance equation, if viewed retrospectively.
Waiting for the impermanence of outer space,
the dark star tranquillity

that accompanies your presence.
Methods to provoke misrepresentation
and general ambivalence.
The clear wreckage of afterthought.
Devout trespassing of the inevitable word.

4

The new line gathers and distributes its portents.
The first phrase bereft of promise
sets indifferent channels at odds.
Phantom light supplies the dawn its several hues.
Patterns of emotion trade tragic consequences.
Brightly enclosed and variously constructed
national alarm whimpers a possible variant.
Ancient discontent and forgotten motive
transferred as senseless brooding.
The day enters to close sporadically across
the lettuce patch green in my mind's eye
colour of outrage waste and abuse; theoretically.
Blind too in all that seeing, all those obvious
demonstrations of clarity.
The understudy requires direction.
I lived there frequently left frequently returned
although it remains a mysterious and formal space.
Ask to dream however and there is considerable dissent.
Information highway code retrieval manic programme.
One line the one we all know descent, heritage,
definition, oblique between two points unfixed
and wandering in luxuriant appraisal.
The horse bears her terrifying presence
through the village crimson lips and powdered face
eyes confused by monstrous wit
sensitised in furtive pain.
If she speaks expect to see a toad between her lips.
Phantom light across the shoulder.
Oblique line to bereft promise.
This where I was to this alternative with directions.
Presentation of syllables of lines running.

Should it have been the mad woman finally speaking
who would expose that time for what it truly
might have been.
The dry sparkling scarlet jewel of a mouth
lipping the absence of her death as it leaves there.

5

Demands action. Breath a faint continuation
of the date. Stop.
Charmed, outstretched, dazzled.
That familiar face beyond the energy field
has lived before. Trapped by previous example.
Fill in the forms fill in the forms.
No title, no name. Obliterate difference.
Living here with loose objects.
A room constructed and demolished against a wall
of standing darkness.
Sense creates its own surface into which
you are granted access.
Pass to the embrace of a misguided future.
Realm of an uninhabited land.
Christened a name without substance,
faint growth in contours behind the eyes.
and sometimes to contemplate connections.
Seemingly exclusive, repeating, a command
ignored, associated with a real name.
Were there.
Multiplication of ordinary gestures.
Trees buckle and lurch to appease the storm.
You are missing.
Mind occasions such conjecture.
One road. Memory fanned like a sure hand
of aces.
Voices given strength beyond reason,
I bring you this place. It angels in hours
before speculation.
Truth as a knot falling to moments
of discord filtered through language.

Might be there yet. Sensed also
as multiple. One there attending home,
another seeking reward, retribution, escape.
Another seeking words of compliance
and don't move, magic numbers.
A line balanced at the rim of sleep time.
An order against which to specify and speculate.
From which to extract energy
and by so doing embrace continuance.
Misguided to future.

6

Fend scorn's chill rinse,
explain yourself explain to me.
Gather requests register concerns
describe intense corollary.
No longer bankable: twentieth century
debit-monger, non-person in the teller-sphere.
Narrator roams freak-zone, curiously at odds,
mumbling and coughing repeatedly.
His hands cover lips turning to clay
against his teeth, mouth and nostrils
sucking dust, dreaming air, losing
as a consequence of displacement.
Border disputes re-fence
with a limiting artillery. Individuals are reduced
to nations queuing
at the department of frontiers, futures and loss.
Direct action. Random death.
It is no longer Spring it is somewhere else.
Translucent skies. Imperfect vacancy.
They turn. Launch the perfect sentence.
They are blessed. They have visions.
Their well-being is a threat.
You are the secluded vantage.
Land harried by contradiction and privilege.
Endless night compels the final account
reinstate order without dictatorship.
The light from stars hurting.
Voice at rest, assessing its value sung.
Progress through quality.
The enigma of silence escaping,
that state of inertia, that memory to which
it will be consigned.

7

Beneath, the city remembers daylight,
turns, releases rivulets of plasma.
Earth churn. Hands lay waste in linen folds.
Like fear, that essence which in winning
to its passing strange delights
prepares for odious and frequent rampage.
Gully speech-litter tongues my channel
breath against stray lip diverted across
sweet flesh. Anxiety collective demonstrates
risk. How best prepare orientation to
the unexpected obliquely inclined.
Face a thought.
Idea capable of infinite duplication.
Mascara frames the staring eye. You stare
because it is your eye.
Face caught in a wall.
Become body and blade, wound and dilemma.
Word to sentence, breath to effort.
The rain falls into the ground, the rain
falls onto your head, the rain seeps between
your fingers as the night fails. That look
washed across your features. Flag a breath.
Take. Hidden city stirring
against that hand.

8

Elaborate charades dupe the merciless fund
of anecdotes. Cut off from fatal blather
the mouth gnaws, fretful and determined
at brief yelps of lurching air.
Nervous but in control the host reels
united with various assemblages, crying
and waving, crying out to be transformed,
re-ordered, defined and memorised into the light.
By these such eclipsed and shadowed actions
The truth is withheld, grief checked
at arms length and the vituperative exchange
counts for bought in such markets.
Bluff then and screw the expected advantage.
Blow hot blow cold in never-never land.
Out there silence reclaims the average muzak
of the malls dispersed beyond reasonable doubt
into the fading graph of empty management.
By this time I had still not entered a city,
and the road came and went in that orderly
exchange of intention. I stepped beside it
relishing the suck of air from passing cars.
Then a question occurs.
These things are known to happen.
Sometimes.
And this question refused to be answered,
stubbornly rejected the possibility of discourse
towards a resolve. A question telephoned
through the airways.
The door stands open against looming decision.
By this time the signals.
By this time the signs and portents.

By this time the satellite communiqués.
The extraterrestrial magic.
The ancient sites of ritual death, modem
to monitor. How scream on the internet,
transmit visions by e-mail.
Bleep God of defunct soul pushed into the blue.
Map strategy fed to mission chief
locking smart bombs through smart-card deficit
and smart-ass tactics onto specific target.
Reshape the damage limitation exercise,
landscape the scorched earth policy drop zone.
So here, memorised in light, staged,
tactics exposed, reciting fatal blather,
driven ashore, wrecked at this stoppage,
perfectly cast, askew.

9

Eternity I enclose this hideous memo,
unfortunate bearer of ill-tidings,
unprepared to fend the hour's pestering,
I expect response from the given quarter,
not the extended contraflow
of mirage nor the irreversible slam
of tragic ordinariness but the shape
the true form of wayward intimacy.
Great dream Sleep off the consequences.
Cast a rune, hum a dumb tune.
I must say this.
Ways to understand
far places, distant land.
That the will to discover exploits
an underlying fear and possession
of this knowledge is like the yearning
to share such tidings and premonitions
as consequence and continuity bedevil us.
Emphatic, like air displaced, rapture
and enchantment, a storm
in outrageous dispute above the meagre shelter
where the first part of this message
dumps its flailing aspirations
in the embrace of silent receivers,
blank screens nudged to life. Take it.
Technology and art fuse.
Cast in the guise of holy reformer.
Repairman agnostic, fuelled with righteous
doubt.
Those waterfalls, the stream and its cleansing
flow, ornamental in a captive state.

New world intricacies. Show me your room.
Convene in the wilderness.
Shape the true form, abide with me, pestering
the hour's nebulous production.

10

A body's singular provenance, palace of silence,
palace of dust. Garden ripped from turf.
Blades, blooms, moments of stillness.
Gross dream product confronts frightened observer.
Envious of such melodramas the curator of pose
plucks late fruit fermenting to mush at a stalk's end,
poised to drip from the bough.
Do you remember standing in an orchard, turning
to face the sun, barely able to maintain
a steady gaze of intention, and when you spoke
seemed hardly real, whose voice breaking
from that distance, breaking effortlessly,
caused immediate loss. Probably. Probably optional.
And spoke for what seemed like a conversation's
worth of programming. These efforts, these intrinsic
parallels beneath a surface of wound gauze
bleak with stain. Cause for imagination's rebuke
to wilful and gratuitous chanting.
Then spoke for a conversation's worth of programming.
And in so doing unmask the true nature of absence
slipping through time and again as though a slight
breeze had nestled against the closed door,
against space scattered with trace elements
of a language. What we might have said. Serial
systems. What might have been said, been tapped onto
the keyboard, wrested through digital auto cue proposal.
An architecture of the age, a suitable ruin.
One night horses you said, horses were running
along the avenues, manes furling, tails lashing, horses
running. And when you reached the corner, street light
opened coils of darkness brightly, glinting stars

retreat seemingly dematerialised, as nothing,
beyond intrusion. Null.
Further, he said. Night air slips, unfolds moves and merges
with disturbing grace. There once more, place of early
yearning against bleak endeavour. Moon. Really silvery
and light. Snow running chill strands across the tarmac.
Appeal of bleating misfortune, bowl of dud fruit,
mulch of neglected membrane, magic a dimension previously
spared a history of absence. Nowhere to go walking
between villages, forgetting, inspired by the difficult
nature of intention. Your face would in silence spell
its heathen warning, awash with radiant subterfuge.
Times of what I find there easily mislaid, tense
but redeemable, offered back, darkest between two points,
one a telephone box the other of reference. Light thing
that might be. Account dispatch and fade. Skin penetrates
slightest movement, hands melt on sheets of discarded
calculations. The buzz of symbols tormenting perfect solution.
Make way regardless. One road. Seamless gratification.
Distract and divert. Status outcome. Awakening crisis
salute that name in light.

Delight's Wreckage (2001)

Shining Channels

SHOAL

From flare to blur sharp coastal light
passes with a nod
this side a magic line, drawn in sand
lost in tides.
Invisible trajectories exploit
the still clear water, absorbed by placid deep,
traced on spectral charts
explicit and dissolving,
teased by gusts of dry summer air,
sentenced to explain.
Shoals flex and twist the fretful currents.
Surface tension segregates the random influence
of a hand sampling water
from the muscular twitch of shining fins.
At land a valve opens.
Air bleats at what it fails to circumscribe.
It has its orders.
Horizon, a line of convenient exchange,
remembers to be there.
Unlike a name exhaled against sea change.
They gather and disperse beneath a surface.
They are supreme,
balanced in water, sliding through light,
assembling and fragmenting the name
where it precedes a breath, a slight pressure,
an atmospheric shift. Impossible to contain,
its image retreats through shadows on water.
Forgotten response,
a loss of purpose, the failure of intent

Interval

Return to be there to attend to arrive there.
Shining channels. Metallic folds.
To arrive. To return. To be there.
Action reconciles the interval.
Opulent leverage. Dashing gusts. First to be reminded
then to pause. Taste enduring air. Return
to attend. Shining channels engage the interval,
emphasising choice.
Controlled farewell.
First discover anew, short-circuit the pause.
Change is one thing then it is another.
Aggressive gusts ruffle leaning sails.
Day picks up where it was left. It is not the same.
One thing then another.
Attend something otherwise engaged.
Be there. Recognise the interval and leave.
The language of trade and barter. After the pause
the waiting. The hint at something other.
Cavern of stale sighs. Brief engagement.
Shadows on a far slope, wandering, dissolving.
It follows that the instruction remains.
It follows that the land has re-opened its wounds.
The colours and the light are familiar
to a past and its variable density.
Your last salute and curious changes.
Darkness central to all light.

Dead Letter Drop

Facts assign a particular quality
Capable of withstanding examination,
Unmediated, remarkable and platonic.
On the other hand movement in its simplest state
Disturbs the longing for investment.
Intuition sets a template against flawless form.
Strict contradiction ordained to challenge and usurp.
Such fascination with catastrophe.
So speculate on exotic revelations
That immodest expansion
Through sedimentary haze.
An invitation precisely assembled,
An answer to mock unsavoury reserve
Crawled free of sleep's mansion.
The morning activates its process,
All windows thrown wide to catch the hesitation.
Something new passing through chance remarks
Lines jettisoned from rooftops
One block east of Central Park, severely shaken
By hurricane winds at the edge of expectation.
Closets of musing fog, dull omens, dispersed
Intelligence, lost information
Out-manoeuvred by the wreckage of a sentence.
Its value retained.
What it surrounds and how achieving such a state
Might add to the nature of its alliance
With that unflinching gaze,
Beset as it might seem, beyond us now.
The effort to unmask dissent
An error of space.

Shift

Savannah soul uncoils through regions lacking frontiers
Vestigial guilt falters where music encourages a promenade
So this is summer anointing with its tropic sheen
A coarse wing passing before shadows signals absence
Where you walk the brittle terrain lizards dart
Between rocks and a snake slides like mercury in the heat
Of your bloody heartbeat the pale debris of desperate regard

REVISIONARY

Encoded by default
The page employs our service
Multiple variations progress a splendid discourse
Its colourful diversities and memorable twists
As rancour begets barren response
So too the wake of aimless deduction signifies
Each fluctuation the absent other transcends
Token lamentations, colder than your eyes display,
Confound such massive impertinence
Between the late shift and the early risers
A veil of bilious stars descends
And disappears while we wait to join the day
Headphones lie aside
Bereft of power, silent
A reprieve culled from malicious reference
Whose sweet alternative, emergent grief,
Samples the destructive pause
An addendum, a fluent index, makes useless offerings
And crippling retribution dissolves in risen light

The Excommunicant

Everlasting blue profiles noxious air
A changeling examines residual stuff
Carried in the civilised ballast of progress
Vegetation settles to rot
Osmotic regeneration classifies the mulch
Of querulous exposure
Polluted sighs haunt pungent air
Where the clatter of an electric storm
Gains impetus
Time without day without night without end
Its lingering reproach that binds
Impulse and reserve to the driven form
Of reaction
Field of light everlasting, implacable, vindictive
Field of ancient light
Oracular influence
The rapid sweep of sub-atomic time fields
The post-operative blur of chance moments
As in the legacy of fictitious data
My apparent delusions, the debris of betrayal
In pursuit, beyond us, disqualified
Knowing such provides suitable
Resistance to sleepless hours
Naming them invites the enemy to partake
Of this strategy
Dream it away, the sky recovers
Without day without night without end

Recoil

Organic shade to deepest green. Tangled fauna
Soil heaving. Damp earth stalls neutral push.
On to clearer space through foliage mantle.
Seek and spread a perfect margin of gymnastic light
On land grown strange to observation's circuitry.
To clearer space. To space of loss less perfectly described.
Cerebral cortex awash with dying insect vibrations.
Action settles to hurt
In cloisters and passageways of ignorant flesh.
The burden of complacent day dispersing odours
That intermingle in the drenched cover of pungent vegetation.
And from that darkest place no sign.
No moment for further contemplation. No mutual salvation.
Ill at ease in that desolate warmth.
That destination, that darkest place.
Stations of awakening flesh. Moment of loss.
Fading in the sinister glow that attends you
In the spun light barely discernible. Something missing
Comes to reside.
Order and distinction attend the margins where arable meets
Woodland and limbs entwine and leaves tongue the shade.
A glaze of irony, certainly the ultimate separation, delivers
Its lunge and final sigh of blunt recoil.
Knowing this to be privileged information, or a hint at least,
One is enabled. Having discarded the blindfold of inevitability
A second chance presents Being and Nothingness
In Rural Bliss. Strange ways no flora can entice to fixate.
Claimed space to rewrite a history of future states

Invisible Detachments

The ritual of subconscious vigilance
Rejoining the performance of the day
You will inhabit,
Alert to its many and peculiar ways.
The absolute, the certain understanding
That vanishes in the sheer tone
Of morning's haunting bell.
That fragment of future present
In the stealthy approach
Of dawn's first glance.
Momentarily aligned in the absolute
And certain understanding of nothing
More to add.

Where Once Was

FURTHER INSTRUCTIONS
For Peter Riley

From nothing. For nothing prepares a path
more pathological than loam, than darkness.
True earth. What lies. What lies in wait is the lie
of the land, crowned in copper light. Light sloping
over a ridge pulled free, pulled from free air.
Resolve. Resolve never to repeat, return.
Resolve never to return. To retrace. Never to retrace
The lie of the land. Lost light. Last rays slipping.
Slipping to overcast. As though to return but not
here. As though to depart, but another place
As though arrive, but without announcement. As though
from nowhere. From where loam and darkness conjoin.
It is something and nothing prepares. For nothing.
To arrive. Depart. Retrace.
Resolve never. To repeat return but not here
For nothing prepares for lies. For life. To act.
To act upon the moment's discourse. Discovery. Resolve
response. The world outlines its utterness.
Utterance to circumscribe the world's unqualified
lineaments. To state discovery as its journey.
As though return bore likeness but not familiarity.
To repeat. For nothing. For nothing but the ability
to confront. Slipping light.
The instrument of response through knowledge.
As though another place. Here. As though controlling
divine fragments in unlimited resolve. As though
thought. Ascendant spatial matrix of engagements.
Thought, response, the instrument.
Vast expanse. Language and silence. Confrontation.
Luminous planes buckle urgently.

Moves

Air.
An air of latent menace confronts oblivious advances.
Defence attacks despair. Advance warnings recoil
from charades of brittle light, the lingering heatwave
expires. A name seeks to be announced, owned.
A name seeks its host. Oblivious advances recoil.
Advances wrought from latent menace. A name
encircles the advancing wishes of a former self.
A former self introduces an unknown factor. To seek
its host, a name confronts latent menace.
Tomorrow's stroke of indecision informs today.
A heatwave proves its fickle nature
advancing no particular theory. No theory attached
to the strain of despair. A name remarks.
Menace confronts oblivion. Sentimental to the last.
The name naming. The name named. The name spoken.
Despair banished, menace maimed.
Heartache is a pumping station under stress.
Melancholy Lane is a no through road.
Redeemed. Redeemed by chance. The unknown factor
descending from archaic heights. By chance
the name remarks. The remark lingers, advances,
recoils. Advances, lingers and adopts its host.

INTERROGATION

Engaged. Engaged in calling, the voice is released.
The voice is released forever. Released into cross currents
and exhalations. Into the discharge from monstrous
ventilation ducts. Into mobile air. Notice the music
of the teeming streets. The responsibility of disobedience.
Notice how in a quiet way, how it has disturbed
the drift. The drift and tremor of its own preamble.
Street corner logic. Pavement disguise. Pavement in
Disguise. Notice the unspoken exchange. Transference.
The disguise that promises. The unchecked movement.
Notice the disguise.
The disguise that hints. The certainty of clear high notes.
Clear high notes sung to teeming streets. Cross rhythms
and quiet exhalations. Begin to doubt. Enter. Enter
of your own free will. Notice I am you. You are the narrator.
Caught in momentary disbelief. Before departing. Forever.
Before departing forever. You call. When you call. When
you acknowledge receipt. Notice how notice is given.
Am I the implement you ask. The question. Not when you call.
Not in a quiet way. When you call. Certain, meticulous,
Exploring. How boundaries cease. How boundaries cease
to restrain. How when you call boundaries cease to restrain.
How boundaries in disguise no longer convince.
No longer convince or cease to contain. Convince or cease.

Thomas's Splint

A fracture. Multiple bone fragments. No pin
or plate appropriate. Appropriate or capable
of assembling to realign the shaft.
To contain the spread. Arrest dispersing stress.
Muscles and tendons. Ligaments and flesh.
Combining to contain. Combining to distort.
Distort with variable stress. Neither pin nor plate.
No open wound to access the ruined site. Dissimilar transactions.
External manipulation to recreate damaged structure.
Damaged structure of a principal shaft. Principal
shaft of bone. Rubble of fragments realigned.
Original shaft ghosted. Rubble of fragments. Packed.
Packed and wrapped. The limb packed and wrapped.
Attached within an iron frame. Timber post supporting
iron frame. Weighted in proportion to the trunk's anchor.
Tractive force. Steel timber and flesh.
Stillness. Inertia. Waiting matched
to callus formation. Callus formation. Neither pin nor plate.
Grey callus shadow to white calcium control.
Predetermined duration. Prognosis: to preserve
or amputate. To amputate or persevere. Quality control
of healing. The nature of adjacent damage.
Variants of related conditions. Infection and
Deterioration. The unpredictable nature of the host.
Hostile complications. Antibodies. Fluids. Defender
of the process. Defender against irreconcilable failure.
Adjacent condition.
Defensive process. Garrison of flesh on alert.
Joint adhesions—Nerve repair—Healing damage.

A Rant

And always the truth. The truth
like morning hauled from darkness. Hauled from
darkness. Hauled and cast across the shadowed city.
You go. You stay. It is late. The dull contest
of these sentiments. These sentiments cast across
the mind. It is late. You go. Shadowed by sleep.
By dreams remembered. Remembered and forgotten
In the narrow system of dawn's replenishment. A refrain.
Forgotten. Forgotten by the tongue. The tongue that
lashes within its sour box. To catch a word. A word.
A word foresworn. On and on. You go. You stay.
The silence slips. Slips away. Limbs gather and articulate.
The mist rolls forward, squandering its pithy screen.
Squandering its pithy screen on surfaces ablaze
from rising sunlight. Rising light. The words go on.
The ways made clear. Clear light into turmoil.
Clear light into the turmoil of day. You go. You stay.
And then dreams again. Never to be. Never to be
remembered. Pushed aside. Incurious thing.
The troubled silence without its prompting. The wish
to go. Never to be. Made clear. To go. To go on.
The truth's predicament. Never to be. Never to be
silent. And always.

RITUAL

The mundane business of a line advancing. A line
advancing. If a line is what went by. What went by.
What is spoken. In your absence. Absence counts
on your discretion.
If a line went by. A line went by.
To prevent the destruction of children. How they bear
the pain of our folly. The pain of our folly. How we
carry that negative image. Project that negative image.
Knowing to pronounce where we came from. To own that place.
That place of ritual conflict. A burden of malleable images.
Pronoun imprint. A repetition of lives. Layered hurt.
How it moves. Travels to and fro. There and back. Away
and here again. Pronounce where we come from to such a place.
Open for business social insecurity. Defrayed with cant
and further cuts. Blade to a dull place. Diagram of sharp
relief. No name to inflict. Optimism dispersed at a stroke.
Name of dismantled elements. Solar gleam.
The clean incision of language. A line. An entire life
begins. An entire line begins. From a dull place
to a solar gleam. Home of the senses. A line from here
to where. An entire line to such a place. Such a place.
Such a place illuminated by a solar gleam. From a dull place
to solar gleam. The business of a line advancing.
A line to where. An entire line to such a place.
Advance into solar gleam.

Passages

PASSAGES

   There are no beginnings.
In the finale, no end. There is no
end, no beginning, to assuage.

   The night grows warmer, rain moves
to each moment, beginning and ending:
ending to begin again. The stealth
of passing time, as though these words
marked each encounter, as though
each encounter might be the last.
Words between beginning and ending.

   Ruins on a plateau of broken legislation.
In the end no finale. The mind of the keeper
of donations squandered, whose sentence
is silence, whose policies bereft, whose
destination a far place, in a kingdom
of dreadful neutrality,

   between beginning and ending, weariness,
debate. An opal twilight statistically barren.
No, no beginning. Yes, no beginning,
no end.

CAMOUFLAGE

Sequence and consequence.
Intentional camouflage.
Folds of meaning. Fields of enlightenment.
Alert in a place where nothing happens.
Fields of sound folds of light.
Procedures undone in the wake of passing.
Nothing happens. Ways of advancing retrieved
from a torn landscape, fragmented histories,
challenged hearts. Dream time alert
on perfunctory ground. To have remained.
Never to arrive. Lost orders, bogus portfolio,
deformed heart. Alert in a place where nothing
happens. No ordinary dispatch.
Peevish cries of a majority. Dream time vagrants
reaching through space/time continuum
to tell of a name beyond recall.
A name to subvert meaning.
Text envy in an arms race beyond reach.
Outstretched wings that maul the dubious thermals
pumping freakish energy
through atmospheres of perfect summer day
to raging gale, or missile fall-out dumping
fire on the swollen drop zone.
Fields of light fold in.
Last ardours of a deformed heart.

FINDINGS

It is an unseasonably mild December night, without frost
and moist from contrary winds.

If this is our due, our just deserts, we are done for.

Applause ripples like a wave tilting, a breeze in raucous,
leafless branches.

You walk across the square. Across the empty square.

The paving is dry. Dry and brushed and clear of debris.
A small box slides and rolls towards you. Slides and rolls
and stops. Slides and rolls towards you. You stop.

You stop in the shadow of the railings that surround
the garden. Nothing moves. The wind falls away to stillness.
Stillness transfixed. Nothing moves.

There is a sound. There is a sound like voices.
Like voices fading. Voices fading in a vast auditorium.

At the four corners of the square four figures appear,
simultaneously. Four figures appear and walk briskly along
each side of the square. Along each side and away
into the dark streets surrounding.

Then you move. You move. Continue to walk across the square.
Continue on your way. On your way again,
towards your destination.

MASQUE

The weight of discourse, its consequence.
Language
that transforms. A universal mechanism
Startling illuminations,
swiftly
exposed to manipulation.
As waves unwinding,
no return.

Sweat slick over cold flesh.
Full moon warped by hypnotic fog, moving in darkness,
silent
and conforming to atmospheric demands.
Pushed aside where it might lie
in the flimsy haze of a day sent clean.
Foreign exchange and inevitable consequence.
The currency of disaffection.

Many descriptions made possible,
Your dress not one of them. Making the sign of touch.
Many words less than silence.

Exchange of yearning signals. A beacon torched into
the darkness. Thought shifts declining this desirable
state of engagement. Pink afterglow.
Brilliant line
unclaimed. How many voices, how many voices calling.

Wall of what surrounds. Apparatus of falling down.
Consequences gag abridgement. Waves unwinding.
Departures, expressions of regret,
instances of failure to engage.
Other tributes.

The silliness of air, columns rising from grass, water
at once refreshing and flamboyant; reserved, beyond reach.
Familiar in dreams, lost from memory, stored
in the language particles of progress and dissent.

ANCIENT WISHES

What is visible remains so after the advance of twilight and a deepening sense of loss invade the extraordinary fabric a sentence bestows.

You struggle to avoid the personal but expect to appear as an image on the retinal backdrop. As in, echoing chambers, damp embraces, light through body hair.

Something lyrical. Stars rehearse beneath a proscenium arch of ancient wishes. Technology stuns alien crystal cupped in stone. Leaves unfurl, unforgiving, to fretful air.

Astride a tropic line chance encounters advertise the commonplace.
North or south is of little consequence, stamina remains a potent force. Blue. Quick. Regulated. Necessary influence.

You have discovered a language at large in a place dedicated to deciphering the complex proposals of ancient wishes. Their history,
its outcome, our needs.

As in retribution falling upon us from the noisy chapel pulpit as we prayed to passing time, accelerate; to light, explore these hideous polished shadows; expression, achieve an utmost clarity of savage proposition. To fill the babbling mouth with self-loathing
and extreme humility, to close the lid on this voice box, undo status, revert to complexities of pleasure and technology.

Variations

ANCIENT WISHES 2

Phantom stars rehearse their future
Those preparing and those long ago departed
Those whose presence reassures and those forgotten
Alien crystal stuns the enquiring eye
Foliage reflex frets in sudden air
Unforgiving light
A place inverted for such transactions
Star screen charts movement in an estimation
of intent and how we partake seemingly enclosed
in the delirium of speculation
The delirium of considering
what may not exist, deciphering ancient wishes
What may not exist in our fragile lives
laying down its musculature
A sum of parts that move   move and respond
respond and grow old here
Dead stars fulfil their ancient promise
Visible but silent without language
an eternal state of constancy rendered perfect
and renewed
Random silent without boundary
Which will be forgotten which will exist forever
Which will exist condemned
in time's dead starless night
Silent, cold, embraced by classics from technology
and the arts.

FRAGMENT

Bone white summer sky.
Thunder's far remonstration.
Shouts sirens worthless encores.
Chill after sudden rain,
damp lilac,
the smell of damp lilac.
The pungent smell of wet stone
and wet sand.
Chill air, invigorating air.
Distance intrudes like memory.
Day begins and day ends.
Ends. Begins with the colour of absence.
The stillness of death's blood,
rock brittle earth
and rancid pain.
Sound of voices. The echo
of the sound of voices
telling of those who fled.
Sound intrudes like a memory.
Fleeing plague. Another time.
A distant place considered safe,
thought immune.
A cruel blight. The funerals continue
month after month.
Names appear above doors, letters cut
into lintels.
Their day ends. Time passes.
Nauseating smell of wet earth,
of damp stone and green stuff.
A crow stoops oblivious over carrion,
wings outstretched, plucking entrails,

delving at the core, at the emptiness
of what happened.
A hand strokes a distorted face,
fingers cross the eyelids,
ruining the sun.

INCIDENTAL

And be submerged by envious shade, impotent
dark embellishment. Current loss in wire traceries
rising to vacant spillage, invisible surge
through shapely filaments, subdued light
and invincible hum. Generator's siren song unheard,
out of range, lost.
To falter but not yield. Almost but not surrender.
Not succumb. Acknowledge essential radiance, pause,
losing familiar currency.
The time it takes to say so.
That this exchange predominate.
"I am only heartbroken in the
Victorian sense."
A flawless breeze spreading sheets
of sluggish absence to numb the power of sleeping
warriors. Awake they fret that their next stanza
might slip the page.
Almost but not surrender. Submerged
but never forgotten. Absent though entirely concurrent.
Power's urge feeds wasted wires knotted as a bangle.
Images of interference across the glowing
screens of industrial contrivance.
A rehearsal, disappointing though complete
explores a planetary chart for favours, clues,
an expedient. Wild light running.
What we have lost, where we cannot be,
its forsaken promise.

VARIATIONS

Granite glistens where light lies idle.
Absorbed, caught and thrown.
Caught, held and thrown.
All is still, seems to pause.
High bright and glowing in azurine twilight.
Dance steps turning.
The moment's advantage a sweet glissando.
Mind to momentum aimed and released.
Stillness preparing. Impulse relentlessly
diagrammed. Dancing mottles air.
Unlimited calculations expelled to silence
through evasive recall. This is the twist
and it goes like this. Only relent.
Persist to inexorable conclusion.
Effort as needs be. Succession a distance
controlled and lost. Effort claimed
to maintain self's control.
A moment's concentration from future
time lapse inhibition. Refrain, rhythm
and motion, dancing on a shadow's rim.
Glittering hard micaceous light.
Vapours wiped clear by heat's edge.
Summit of ruffled air. Interrupted rhythm,
expelled breath, slipstream hiss through
golden air. Resilience, tenacity and devotion.
The art of leaning. The tug of speed thrown
into ratios of turning and perilous descent.
A moment of absence passing through
the lacerated surface of stillness.
Absolute stillness to perfect glissando.

BREAK

    Cool translucent June days. Opaque sky.
The flawed rim of a cooling tower obliterated by vapour.
Invisible words. Resting on the lips of an open mouth.

    Glazed dawn, slick moist and ruinous silver.
June days as they never were. Calendar of time's retreat.
Memory yet to be. Warm later like words from other days.

    The exquisite rush of time. To touch
where limbs attach. Armpit, shoulder, hip and groin. Occluded
front. Lip of high pressure zone in time-bound observation.

    Always were. Breath drifting on waltzing tongues.
One into another to the next invisible horizon.
Cool summer evening. Crisis dissolving to anxiety.

    Listening to divine voices. Memory erased so.
Appropriately placed. Energy seeping into the object
whose name remains unspoken. Summer but flawed.

    Hat pulled down lest it float from the skull
into June sky's remarkable spread. Magritte could.
Pause to voice future injunctions. Peripatetic announcement.

    Will break away. Flawed. To drift without purpose
among the target's maze of deceits. Opaque to a point. Lost.
Signal of breath. Cloak of noise. Invisible words lipped to air.

AT WARREN STREET

Blood on the floor
on the grey terrazzo steps
for no apparent reason
trampled to a film
a smudge transferred
to other destinations
Wind barely audible
you did not forget
loose nudge rising and collapsing
through the streets
you remember
sparse but drenching rain
fallen to cease
a bright star
beyond the moon's effervescent light
and a voice calling
Hey! Hey . . .
invading the general hum
Dull red footprints
on grey terrazzo
were there you turn
at the sound of steps
in an underpass
where was that
the echo of a voice receding
The rain stopped if you were there
wind in retreat and the voice
diminishing there
if at all

ECHO

There were many alternatives.
The way they might fold in and out against the pull
of lunar flexing.
Bright they might be, drifting through towers
of oxygen, simple beads hung in water.
Numbers escape to air.
We are done with counting. Dry summer
gusts haunt the surface of water.
Gulls clamour and appear indifferent.
The elaborations of such exotic creatures,
wary, suspended, impress the eye.
Who surround islands, construct reefs,
develop whole continents of meaning,
floating free before our watchful conceit
sucking air, blowing air, suffering light,
suffering blades of light,
lost in seeking a name.
Once you thought to touch cool scales,
a shining flank, sense the tremor
of lacy fins. But this was illusion,
a counter-claim of water dripping
from empty fingers, describing a sensation,
an amazement, a curiosity of light
borrowed from shadow, from sea-change,
a twist and dash of perfect enshoalment
lost in your absence.

DEEP PILE

There is a place called home.
There is a place called home to some.
Green onyx, amber stone, subliminal guilt.
There is a place called Deep Pile.
Nothing escapes. Obsidian paraphernalia.
Obscene retribution.
Radio telescopes tilt
to confront deep space.
Signals from far memory patterns.
Through the click and electric chatter
of meteorite showers.
Cruising for the charged embrace
of summer night transmission phases.
Shades of erotic satin. Sunlit water
running over coral beds.
The Dralon folds of sound-waves
endlessly moving.
The rough abrasive quality of that touch.
Artificial stone terraces
bereft of fossil trace.
Memory consummated in air
where flesh attends flesh.
A place called dense retreat, home to some.
Green onyx. Deep Pile.
Nothing.
No one escapes.

Elsewhere in Disguise

COMMERCIAL BREAK

In a town not chosen for its charm
rain falls from the overcast
adding heedless verve to the general smear
Composite themes and separations
identify choice of solitary awe
and fabulous complicity exhaled
like a breath unmeasured across
the tongue's slick of melting acid bile
through lips that shape words
from the desperate silence of indifference

Legend of descending moon distorted
Dripping walls trap light loops
Water buckles the lurching image
torn from a father's dreams revealed
where cars chide the curb's black step
Names mentioned fade on stone
and the other stands for no good reason
but to turn elsewhere in disguise
from a place like that to another day
moved one hour on in summer time

Dogmatic national grid terminates delirious
in a concentration of myriad lights
scattered across glistening industry
a moment's casual ease reciting
the appointment of demon legislation
Smart talking sustained because desire lurks
because repeat cancelled nation carelessly turning
Movement of compromise and error of judgement
A blue gown billows to the common ground
furls open empty and yielding

In memory of failure unprepared to rejoice
abuse directives and misuse charts
Query historical accuracy such places expose
Rummage in corners bewildered forsaken by truth
Waxed awnings snap in wind unharnessed
Full air blowing rank and littered obnoxious
Love and death and far light perpetual
misguided but open to interpretation
left far behind striving for the unattainable
No compromise Certain absence
Unwanted legacy

SUB-TROPICAL GARDEN
for Lucy

Resolute and courageous,
gold, orange and scarlet ciphers
code the water,
 dispersing silver splinters
beneath a taut overlay
of meniscus grip.
You describe their circular pathways,
syllables of translucent motion,
punctuation in a gasp of delight.
Your hand dips into the speckled surface
like a fairy tale mirror
access to parallel text, a door opening
against all odds: lock, bolt, catch,
a tilted chair.
Surface set in motion by probing fingertips.
A maze of branches buckles
on the resting sky reversed
between polished leaves of lilies
nudged by clouds
and the held edge where outstretched ripples
bounce, self cancelling.
Mandarin and cadmium flecked water
dashed and dissolving its pattern
like cracked glass repairing, a wound
healing, a door closing in silence.
Wearing garments of pleasure,
you run from the dancing pool
through tangled shrubbery
and humid air, answering
the peacock's eerie cries,

the splendid apparatus of discerning wisdom.
Adrift on ripples in extraordinary confusion,
you are smiling and learning
and all that surrounds and follows you
yet to be assimilated or deferred.

AIRING

The ways and some of their versions
some speak to you
some arrive between the rains
and some note the changes there
Some additional elements
and some remarkable transactions
Some in context some to be placed
Some to repay old debts and some to remind
of the original impulse
Those who work there and those
who honour the fugitive dead
Some of the pain and some of the absence
Some of the means and some of the end
Some who are informed
and some who know otherwise
Some who are making for the borders
and some who loiter still
in rooms overlooking
a deserted square
Some are assured and some miss the point
Some of the future
and some other place
Indisputable facts and divine guidance
Some of those and some of that
Some to the distance some of the migrant commotion
some of the far places
some of the nameless and some of the fear
accompanying that anonymity
Some who have walked through the ruins
and some who have demanded the impossible
Some who are present at the chance meeting

some of the literal expression
that we might allude to
The exercise and its outcome
The salute and the approbation
Some of the stories yet to be told
and some of the events that matter
what is to be and what will remain of its passing
What will remain here
Some to tell and some to watch disperse
in fragments

NO NAME

Meticulous surgery at the fault line
Exploratory turmoil
Opening destructive research
Catalogue of wreckage
Breath delivered from lung warmth
Defiance in what you say
Spikes of fire
Lamentations in ash
Fault line of human interference
Across a plateau's uncertain deviation
Between blackened walls
On a dominant terrain
Fault line to the ancestor
Elevated in catastrophic surgery
Ancient celebrity draped with strands
Of decomposing organzine
Lines ideas and legislation
Language waking current events
Exposed to unrapt eyes
The sun at its zenith jubilant
Aura of liberated signals
On the porous surface of occasional delight
Fades in spasms
And the howl of language waking
The interpretation of a chorus waking
A table of damaged signs

SONG FRAGMENT

Words of conjecture spoken
against division and no hope
The only way a wayward tendency
The theory of a foregone conclusion

The verse in adverse conditions
written to receive
Spoken to challenge pause to hear
the alarming signals

Fragile membrane
The absence of the one departed
that remains and continues
Thy silence and thy presence

The undulating waves that transport you
Who leaves is carried from that
which remains by continual reference
to counterfeit images

Menace of a precious slip dormant touch
Thy presence and thy silence
reconcile the unknown that it might appear
in writing in triplicate

A copy for each and a copy
for the dead file that fades when exposed
to scrutiny
That becomes the essence of thought

disconnecting

Marking the Blue

FOR

Alerted to stop.
Nomadic mind trace lately dreaming
fortune's definition outlined
by alchemist bankers,
dealers in stocks and bonds,
peddlers of potions and powders,
the ragbag of monetarist traders and policy-makers.
A course magnificent in natural geometry.
A geometry of accurate form and inertia.
A geometry as like geography
as might seem coincidentally acceptable.
Away from memories.
Obliterating one by one.
Uncomfortable landscape, mark the day.
As gathering storms bruise a pliable screen.
Here where not to be.
The markets shifting.
Transitional states fed to the voracious mouth of mimicry
that it might dispatch silence
with a word.
The word is the one that fits.
Raise your eyes by implication. God as supreme being
acts his curious charades.
Reclaim disguise.
Obscure the frequency yet to transmit.
O legends and angels, the remorseless seem so resourceful.
A missile tracks its prey angelicly, artfully,
without consideration.
No place cooler than this night.
No place where it is not.
Fire's immaculate annihilation. Breath of bitter release.

To connect and wake the roar of impact.
To wake the roar. Intrusion and disturbance of sound.
Phoneme of the language of quenched flame.
Hope extinguished in the communion of exchange.
Object and subject seek to connect,
Strain and expand in mutual regard.
Chance locations, intolerable defeat.
Slow spiral away.

NAMING

Precious day revises judgement,
suspends belief in favour of comparison
to the slow wake of ragged storm.
No word to phrase this canon.
No name.
No future exchange supported by this quest
for keen response.
Each movement determined by the space
it leaves like ripples
on impatient water.
The story telling itself for its own end.
Shadows liberated from their object.
Words agitate the languorous tongue.
No future equivalent.
No present to be so.
Each breath launching a sentence
that fades through the darkness
on a window catching summer light.
The space it leaves
for its own end.
Surface of fused particles blank
with sinuous revisions where a name
we cannot read
informs the shadow's legacy
of no present standing.

RUSE

The hum of the slipstream
of cathartic wind activates nerve terminals
dispersed beneath the skin.
The synthetic the digital the monitored hum.
Empty mutable wind traversing barren landscapes.
Starshine on the heartland.
Dispatches from that quarter,
from that aleatoric spasm.
The vivid the remote the colourless starshine.
The climate of dangerous enthusiasm.
Particular virtue. Archaic privilege.
Vivid remote and colourless in the ferment.
Choral chant to comatose countdown.
Starshine on the harsh lands.
Remarks that clarify and reconcile.
Warnings that recoil. Echo management.
Listen to the hum.
Sentences of explanation. Frail judgement.
Real terms. Peculiar hiatus.
The sustained fragile hum.
The engulfing the quenching the consuming deletion.
The scream that erupts.
The curve of ruinous pain.
The cry. Intervention and survival.
The reverberation of repeated salvoes.
Subdued ripples. Resonating air.
The cadence of an irrepressible hum.
Last sound to be heard. Last audible sound.
Vacant barriers last obstacle.
Enter the slipstream. The wake of birth and death.
Necessary transformation.

The silence of the heartland,
the hum of the voices of the corrupt lyric.
Last sound to be heard.
Last audible sound.

REPAIR

Decorated earth.
Arranged stones in a landscape
artfully raised.
Narrative infiltrates fragile consequence.
Discord rejoicing.
Obligation fabricates change.
Lavish scenes form a backdrop,
dark earth and damp air glittering,
dead fires spontaneously igniting,
confetti of ash and smoke
wreathing the fraught trees.
Disturbed index impressed on furrows
and slopes. Layers blur.
Overprint clamour of encroaching wilderness.
Decorated earth, discordant air.
Insect semaphore laid siege
by ancient fires.
Craters, scarps, distorted ox-bows.
Seasonal cover pealed away.
Miscellanies of fossil debris
orphaned by time.
Silt and marl
inherit captive remnants.
Embalmed pathways, track inheritors
clay and bone in perfect lamination.
Compass turning a magnetic dance.
Mineral light-force rekindled.
Bright sky resumes its day.

CHRONICLE

To rest a weary head on the casual shoulder
of indifference is no mean feat.
No feeble rebuke would have it otherwise.

Distinguished emissaries devise a register
of particulars and name them
Grief, Boredom, Longing and Remorse.
That the list is lost says more than less.

The dead are fearless however, and their absence
remains in the lives of others.
Doors clap enthusiasm for passing numerous souls
entering the fruitful exchange
of this fecund day.

Primed air lingers in the cavities of their repose
as it might falter
before the first moves of a working day
breach its complacent edge
against a body of opinion.

The moon at its third descends
into an awesome obliteration of setting hues,
memorial to the end.
Hold our ground before it shifts,
and walk in the splash of sodium light

through teeming provocative streets
the casual though perfectly clad shoulder
browsing the airwaves.

Delight's Wreckage

Organic shade to deepest green. Tangled fauna.
Soil heaving. Damp earth stalls neutral push.
On to clearer space through foliage mantle.
Seek and spread a perfect margin of gymnastic light
On land grown strange to observation's circuitry.
To clearer space. To space of loss less perfectly described.
Cerebral cortex awash with dying insect vibrations.
Action settles to hurt
In cloisters and passageways of ignorant flesh.
The burden of complacent day dispersing odours
That intermingle in the drenched cover of pungent vegetation.
And from that darkest place no sign.
No moment for further contemplation. No mutual salvation.
Ill at ease in that desolate warmth.
That destination, that darkest place.
Stations of awakening flesh. Moment of loss.
Fading in the sinister glow that attends you
In the spun light barely discernible. Something missing
Comes to reside.
Order and distinction attend the margins where arable meers
Woodland and limbs entwine and leaves tongue the shade.
A glaze of irony, certainly the ultimate separation, delivers
Its lunge and final sigh of blunt recoil.
Knowing this to be privileged information, or a hint at least,
One is enabled. Having discarded the blindfold of inevitability
A second chance presents Being and Nothingness
In Rural Bliss. Strange ways no flora can entice to fixate.
Claimed space to rewrite a history of future states

NOCTURNE

Everlasting residuals of process
reach out to us.
Heaven is the intention of sky.
Scattered suns in glorious star-fields.
Big numbers, celestial names.

Luminous havoc clusters in far space.
Final version that frames
a constellation's brilliance.

No recompense. No comment.

The many suns endlessly moving,
endlessly terminating against our attention,
where it rests in solar dust clouds.
Transmitting past events
to shores of ultra-violet.

Wary eyes focused in deep space.
Eternal showers and turbulent remarks.
Heavenly concerts.

And locate in their emission our source.
Where we were before we pass
to burning dust. We toast your ingenuity,
salute your name which is a number,
a symbol of admissible consideration.
A bright spot expanding,
beyond comprehension, meanwhile

we take air, confirm art,
propose a celebration among footprints
on alien stars,
go immaculate and informed,
exhaling wondrous constellations

EXCURSION

Perverse forms of intention prevaricate

Oral forms determine

No mitigating plea
or justifiable instruction
sanctions rest
that restless continues

But fear not nor acknowledge
Their irascible twists
as rivulets of summer rain cross-hatch glass

Their pattern silently erased in dense heat
Silence unravelling from the heart

The mind's confounded response agog
waiting to return
to be transferred
caught as though about to fall
about to move

When was this of which you speak
Far places restless features

Where are these thoughts to rest
and in repose germinate and shed
their comments

As this day ends in a chance encounter
between strangers following lurid afterglow

Shedding the heresy
of false attachment to previous doubt

FABLE

Limbs commingle ruinously
in silhouette
splay and traverse iridescent space
where bodies fuse
and savage desire
is formally dissembled
Relished by the one who takes refuge
inhabits the pit
stretched on a burning sheet
plunging to mark an impaled husk
Through the gaping pores of isolated
flesh shadow
caught against a wall
Caressing blood rush from regression
Pain of rapid daylight pulse retrieved
Feverish surge
embracing delight's wreckage
Not one image or likeness remaining
Calamitous recitation slips
across the molten tongue
Visions set to slide
the veined and fissured surface
marked by advancing fingers
Renegade contrivance
relinquishing blame
last refuge refused
absorbed in a coherence
of submerged currents
Relished visions quit the feverish pit
never complete
as it gets colder we are further
migrating between facts
extolling the lost cause

DAMAGE FIELD

Desire debates tedious cause. The region is
almost forever. There is a sense of humour.
Tomorrow you will embark. You verify. There is
a portrait concealed in a room to which you are denied
access. Shades click against the open window.
The twist in a version of honesty. A serene
encumbrance. Walls rise into flawless light. White
space exposed in astonishment. Delinquent desires
gleaning residual stuff. Replaying an exquisite threat.
Acquaintance with raw hurt. I write
to you from this far place this adopted land.
Premium of no return. Lines not to be silenced. Fear
named. Dread owning a truth. Written for these
southern shores. Others know by hearsay. The grape vine
potent elixir. In the portrayal you are exposed
to little hope. A way of controlling distance launched
into your sphere. The authorities have been informed.
This could be an end. Rancid loam as far as the eye
will scan. Dark sky altered. This other version surrounds.
There are no absolutes. The veto is complete. The edges
of the canvas are stapled onto the stretcher frame
under tension. No look will develop outside enduring passion.
The years pass. The awkward correspondent, adrift in layers
of meaning, of earthly communication, of paradise
extremes. Me too. Bluff the interviewer. Crack
a smile. Lift a hand. Push a limit beyond question.
Ask it. Objectify idle fears. Who knows. This is a cruel
season. We spread the word the way a tide strokes the shore.
Hope lies
Eternal rest
In peace

CAUSE

Birth membrane shifts
across a bony flange.
Colliding moments
distanced by each dissolving second.

A quote from imminent breath.
Squeals fluctuate through swirling air
not yet in contact, not yet seductive
nor inhaled to launch metaphors.

Though natural recognition
This being small community judgement
Speaks of sin and misses the point

Pale as linen the sky breaks gold
bronze and strained vermilion
watched from a high window.

Spasms regress dark and airless
through divine space. Far empty space.

A donation of speculative disturbance,
without dreams or inconvenient images,
without social awkwardness
or threats of retribution.

The sudden enormity of that brittle room.
The scowl of disguise, the pigment
of narrative composition.

Searching for a phrase, asking a porter,
a news vendor, a fellow traveller.
In some way loss is predetermined,

like a claw grips its prey
a beak of daylight ravages the gloom.

www.ingramcontent.com/pod-product-compliance
Lightning Source LLC
Chambersburg PA
CBHW020217170426
43201CB00007B/239